Praise for
*12 Steps to Having a More Organized
Christmas and Holiday Season*

"I love Christmas, I love family, and I love Lane Jordan's very practical book on how to plan for Christmas. Lane's book will help many of us celebrate this most wonderful time of year in a Christ-honoring and family-strengthening way. I highly recommend this book!"
—**Nancie Carmichael**
Former Editor/Publisher of *Virtue Magazine*
Author of several books including: *Selah*; *Time to Stop, Think and Step into Your Future*; *Surviving One Bad Year*; and *Spiritual Strategies to Lead You to a New Beginning*

"Like Lane Jordan I started to hate Christmas. The busyness and stress stole the meaning right from under me. But in *12 Steps to Having a More Organized Christmas and Holiday Season*, I learned how to let go of the urgent in favor of the important. I was reminded, yet again, about what really matters. Lane helps readers take control of those things we can control and forget the rest. It's never too late to learn how to find joy—the holiday season is a great place to start!"
—**Vicki Caruana**, Ph.D.
Author of the best-selling *The Organized Homeschooler* and *Apples & Chalkdust*

"Lane's book is so much more than the 12 steps she shares with us. Inside these pages she gives us so many gifts: peace of mind, joy, happiness, fun, and freedom. She has handed all of this to us, beautifully wrapped up in her 12 steps and made real with heart-warming stories and real-life examples. All we have to do is "unwrap" them by putting these simple ideas into action."
—**Sandy Fowler**
Creator of the Heart Filled Holidays project
www.HeartFilledHolidays.com

This book, filled with practical and creative ideas, removes stress from the Christmas season. It gives busy women the permission to keep plans and purchases simple, and to focus on what matters most. I wish I'd had this resource years ago!

—**Grace Fox**
International speaker and author of
10-Minute Time Outs for Busy Women

"In Lane Jordan's new book, *12 Steps to Having a More Organized Christmas and Holiday Season*, she will truly help you get organized and de-stressed for the Christmas holidays. With a been-there-done-that expertness, it's obvious her purpose is not just to help you survive a busy season. With practical and biblical guidelines, she'll help you rediscover and enjoy a more meaningful Christmas, with Christ as the true focus."

—**Rebecca Barlow Jordan**
Author of Day-votions® for Women, Day-votions®
for Mothers, and Day-votions® for Grandmothers

"Practical and perfectly delightful! Lane Jordan's new book helps us make it through the holidays with joy and ease. Take it from someone who is not naturally organized, *12 Steps to Having a More Organized Christmas* is sensible and doable. You will truly enjoy your holidays with less stress and more calm with the help of this book."

—**Karol Ladd**
Positive Life Principles, Speaker and Author of
The Power of a Positive Woman

"Lane's new book is a must-have if you want to take the stress and craziness out of your Christmas season. Her 12-step program will not only help you have a more organized Christmas, but help you put the "holy" back into the holiday."

—**Mary Englund Murphy**
Author of *Joseph: Beyond the Coat of Many Colors* and *Winning the Battle of the Bulge: It's Not Just About the Weight*
www.lookingglassministries.com

"With stories and examples, Lane Jordan gives specific, practical applications of her 12 steps to maximize joy and memories while minimizing stress. Any time of the year readers will find *12 Steps to Having a More Organized Christmas and Holiday Season* useful, scriptural, and a fun, easy read."

—**Brenda Nixon**
Host of *The Parent's Plate* radio show, author of the award-winning *The Birth to Five Book: Confident Childrearing Right from the Start*, and conference speaker

"*12 Steps* is a practical resource for those who desire to replace Christmas chaos with organization, clarity, and fun. Lane Jordan shares how to shop with wisdom, prepare a meal that's sure to please, and decorate like a pro. This book will wrap a bow of joy around your Christmas."

—**Laura Petherbridge**
Speaker and author of: *When 'I Do' Becomes 'I Don't' - Practical Steps for Healing During Separation and Divorce* and *The Smart Stepmom*

"*12 Steps to a More Organized Christmas* is just what you need to find the shortcuts that will help you smoothly navigate the busy holiday season. Lane Jordan has thought it through and packs in easy to follow tips and inspiration that will leave you eager and ready ahead of time. Don't give up on the holidays! Lane's book will save the day for a stress-free Christmas this year!"

—**Marcia Ramsland**
Speaker and author of *Simplify Your Life, Simplify Your Time, Simplify Your Space*, and *Simplify Your Holidays: A Classic Christmas Planner to Use Year after Year*
www.organizingpro.com

"Every Christmas I promise myself I'll do better next year . . . and the next year I'm standing in the midst of the Christmas chaos, wondering how I failed again. But with *12 Steps to Having a More Organized Christmas and Holiday Season*, I know this year can be different—even for a domestically disadvantaged woman like me! It's sometimes hard for the Organized to teach the Unorganized of the world. What seems so easy to them can be overwhelming for us, making us feel like failures. But in "12 Steps . . ." Lane lovingly shares her practical suggestions on everything from shortcuts to gift buying and clean-up to outreach, without a wagging finger or a judgmental tone. No guilt trips inside this book!"

—**Vonda Skelton**
Diva of the Domestically Disadvantaged
Speaker and author of *Seeing Through the Lies:
Unmasking the Myths Women Believe* and
The Bitsy Burroughs Mysteries for kids 8 to 13-year-olds

"Lane Jordan gives the word "plan" heightened meaning. Choosing to plan with Lane's 12 holiday steps means choosing blessings for you and all you love. No matter where you turn, you will find an invitation to celebrations of the heart. Her chapter on de-stressing the holidays—with its focus on priorities—is a lifesaver; and her counsel throughout the book is wise, Word-focused, Christ-honoring, and transferable to other areas of life. You will breathe a sigh of relief with each practical tip, and think, 'I can do this, and it will be fun!'"

—**Dawn Wilson**
Founder, Heart Choices Ministries
Co-author of *LOL with God: Messages of Hope and Humor for Women*

12 STEPS

TO HAVING A MORE
ORGANIZED
Christmas and Holiday Season

Other Books by Lane P. Jordan

12 Steps to Becoming a More Organized Woman
12 Steps to Becoming a More Organized Mom
12 Steps to Becoming a More Organized Cook

And she contributed to:
The One Year Life Verse Devotional by Jay K. Payleitner
And
Craft a Life of Passion, Purpose, and Prosperity

12 STEPS
TO HAVING A MORE
ORGANIZED
Christmas and Holiday Season

"This book is just what you need to find the shortcuts that will help you smoothly navigate the busy holiday season." —Marcia Ramsland, speaker and author of *Simplify Your Life*

LANE P. JORDAN

REDEMPTION PRESS

© 2011 by Lane Jordan. All rights reserved.

Published by Redemption Press, PO Box 427, Enumclaw, WA 98022

No part of this publication may be reproduced, stored in a retrieval system, or transmitted in any way by any means—electronic, mechanical, photocopy, recording, or otherwise—without the prior permission of the copyright holder, except as provided by USA copyright law.

Unless otherwise noted, all Scriptures are taken from the *New American Standard Bible*, © 1960, 1963, 1968, 1971, 1972, 1973, 1975, 1977, 1995 by The Lockman Foundation. Used by permission.

ISBN 13: 978-1-63232-051-3
Library of Congress Catalog Card Number: 2010943387

The older I become the more I realize that our life and what we do with it is all about the Lord Jesus. So I dedicate this book to Him and to our Father, Who sent His Son to live and die for us. Thank you, Father, for giving us the best Christmas gift ever.

Contents

Acknowledgments..................................xiii

Introduction xv

The Twelve Steps.................................. xvii

  1. Plan Everything Early 1
  2. Plan Traditions and Memories 9
  3. Plan Your Workload and De-stress Your Stress.......... 17
  4. Plan Your Finances and Buying.................. 25
  5. Plan Your Decorating and Wrapping.............. 35
  6. Plan Your Meals................................ 49
  7. Plan Time for Family, Friends,
     Neighbors, and the Needy 57
  8. Plan Time for Yourself.......................... 67
  9. Plan Time for the Guest of Honor................ 77
10. Plan Time to Reflect and Prepare
     for the New Year.............................. 87

References 97

About the Author 99

Acknowledgments

No one can accomplish their goals without help and support from others. I am not the exception. With the help and guidance of my husband, Scott, I have been able to do the work the Lord has entrusted to me. He has supported me, encouraged me, and been there for whatever I needed. And our daughters, who are the shining lights in my life, have never stopped giving me love, support and their you-can-do-it philosophy. Special thanks to Christi who carefully and beautifully edited this book. Thank you, my precious family.

Introduction

How many of us have awakened one morning only to realize that we have one zillion things to do, by yesterday, because of an upcoming holiday that is *tomorrow*?

Perhaps that example is an exaggeration, but the feeling of being totally unprepared for an upcoming event or holiday is not. The main problem for many of us is that we already are so busy with our overflowing lists that to add just one more thing pushes us to overload.

I remember how easy the Christmas season used to be for me. That is, until I had my first baby and *I had to do what my mother did!* Suddenly, I couldn't figure out when to buy the presents, wrap them, buy the tree, decorate it, make this Christmas full of "special memories," plan the big dinner, cook the big dinner, etc. And it was then that the light bulb of reality was turned on, and I realized that next year, I had better start early!

This book is a compilation of some ideas and successes that have helped me during what is the busiest time of the year for the majority of women—Christmas. Since this is generally the peak time of emotional roller coasters, unending to-do lists, flu epidemics, nativity plays, and children crying, I hope these tips and suggestions will help you, not only during this holiday but also during the other holidays celebrated throughout the year. If you can manage Christmas, other holidays will be tame in comparison!

But remember: all of the activities, trimmings, presents, and meals are really just outward expressions that are surrounding the real focus for the holiday—the earthly birth of God's Son. While the saying may have become trite, Jesus *is* the reason for the season. If we forget about Him on our way to our own "perfection holiday glory," then everything we have done has been done in vain. Yes, the Christ child can be celebrated in a "Martha Stewart Show House," but He also can be celebrated just as well in a hospital room, an airport, a college dorm, a one-room apartment, or even . . . a very small, out-of-the-way stable.

The Twelve Steps

THE FIRST REAL step towards any successful endeavor is deciding what you want. I firmly believe that if you *want* to be more organized, you *can* be, as long as you take the next steps of working hard and seeking out help. I hope that the following twelve steps and ten chapters will be the help you need.

Step 1   Plan Everything Early
Step 2   Plan Traditions and Memories
Step 3   Plan Your Workload
Step 4   Plan Your Buying—Set up a Budget
Step 5   Plan Your Decorating and Wrapping
Step 6   Plan Your Meals
Step 7   Plan for Family—Yours and His!
Step 8   Plan for Friends
Step 9   Plan for Your Neighbors and the Needy
Step 10 Plan Down Time for Yourself
Step 11 Plan Time for the Guest of Honor
Step 12 Plan Time to Reflect and Prepare for the New Year

Chapter 1

PLAN EVERYTHING EARLY

MANY TIMES I am asked what the *number one best tip* is to being more organized. And the answer, though very simple, can be very hard to do. The best tip to being more organized is to *plan*. Plan everything you can, and plan early. This is hard to do because most of us don't even have the *time* to sit down and plan in the first place! And I am with you on that. Most of us don't like to plan. We want everything just to happen. But when we wait for that, nothing will get done. When we plan nothing, nothing happens!

❧ Most of us don't even have the time to sit down and plan. ☙

Some of you reading this book are "Christmasholics"—you love Christmas and wish it could be celebrated every day! Others, like myself, realize how much work, energy, and time it takes to celebrate, and we groan at the very thought of it. (Not the *meaning* of this blessed event, but what it has become.) To many of us, Christmas has become a holiday that makes us say upon its ending, "Next year, I am not going to do all of this again!"

2 · 12 Steps to Having a More Organized Christmas and Holiday Season

Of course, I'm not quite sure what that means—not cooking Christmas dinner, not buying gifts, not decorating? But deep inside, I know exactly what it means. I am rebelling against the feeling of complete exhaustion that the work requires, and that overtakes the beauty and the spirit of why and what we are celebrating. If I can't even sit down and behold the beauty of the newly lit tree or read the story of the Christ Child's birth in Luke 2, then why did I do so much?

For many of us, the holidays are like a faster version of our regular lives. Already busy, we now are adding a whole new list of "to dos" onto an already overloaded to-do list, and we are feeling that mountain of guilt if we don't do it all, not to mention do it all perfectly.

Therefore, this chapter is to help us plan better so that, I hope, we will be able to watch our little ones in their school plays, bake cookies, read Christmas stories, give to others, and above all, remember and celebrate the miracle of God coming to earth as the greatest gift ever given: Jesus, His only Son.

Here are some tips to help you *plan*:

1. As soon as the children go back to school in August, sit down and begin planning where the holidays will be spent. Yes, I know what you are thinking: *August! Why should I start thinking of Thanksgiving and Christmas so early?* Because, the first step to having a more organized holiday season is planning, and planning early. One of the most argued-about parts of the holidays is where you will be spending them, correct? Your mom wants you every holiday but so does your mother-in-law. Your children only want to go visit their *favorite* cousins and not the *other* cousins. If this is a recurrent fight in your family, perhaps you could be the one to set up a schedule. For example, on even years, you go visit one family and on odd years you go visit the odd, I mean, the other family!
2. Another reason to choose the location of the celebrations early is because of travel plans (such as booking airplane tickets), and you will need to make those plans

early. Additionally, it will let you know if you are spending Christmas at home or away, so you can adjust your plans for your decorating, etc. Contact the different family members and try to get an answer as soon as possible.
3. Set a deadline for when you want to be finished with all you want to accomplish for that holiday. This is very important. Setting a deadline gives you a concrete goal that will keep you going in the right direction. For me, my deadline for decorating, greeting cards, and gifts (buying and mailing) is December 1. That may seem early for some of you, but it is actually only twenty-five days before Christmas. If I am finished with my decorating, cards, and gift buying and mailing by December 1, then I am free to really enjoy the celebration! I have time to attend the school and local community events. I have time to bake with my children and give my time to the less fortunate. And I have time to really enjoy the reason for the season.
4. Begin making a master list for other goals you have for this holiday. Set a day for getting your Christmas tree or setting up your artificial tree. If this is the year you want to go out in the country to cut your own tree, begin researching tree farms in your area. However, I don't advise doing this with children under the age of five! Yes, it seems like it would make such a wonderful, "Walton family" memory, but children's attention spans are short, and they don't care where the tree came from. They just want a happy family that is together.
5. If you bake at Christmas for your family and/or for gifts, plan a time on your calendar. That way you can go ahead and purchase the ingredients as well as give yourself an open day so that you don't feel rushed.
6. With more mail coming into your home during the busy Christmas season, plan a "mail station." This could be your desk or a small area in your kitchen where you open the mail *daily* and where you have all the supplies you need right at hand: scissors, tape, pens, paper, address book, stamps,

and a trash can. As cards begin coming in, you can check addresses, in case there are new ones, change them in your address book, and then place the cards in a basket for the family to see. If I am in a hurry, I keep the envelope that has the return address on it and save it in my address book until I have time to check on it, which is usually after Christmas.
7. Begin making a list of all of the gifts to buy. Since this is such a large chore, Chapter 4 will go into more detail on this topic.
8. Plan a place for gifts to be stored in your house. If you have little ones who want to find what Santa is bringing them, this is very important! One of the best places to hide gifts is in a guest shower that never is used, especially if the glass is fogged so that you can't see in. Also, if you purchase gifts throughout the year, make sure you label the bags or boxes with what they are and whose presents they are. Trust me on this one, because six months after buying a gift, a person (myself included) will totally forget for whom the gift is intended!
9. Plan memories. No matter what holiday you may be enjoying, the memories are what will last. I believe it takes time and planning to insure that there will be memories for us and our families. We will go into this in more detail in the next chapter.
10. Plan time for Jesus. This is covered more in Chapter 9.

I'd like to share a story with you. It reveals that anyone, even a princess, can have problems if he or she forgets to plan.

Once upon a time, there was a beautiful princess who lived far, far away in a majestic castle high upon a mountain. She was dearly loved by her subjects, for, besides being beautiful, she also was very kind. In fact, they thought she was perfect in every way.

There was a special holiday celebrated in the land once a year. As soon as the trees began to sprout their new leaves and the flowers began their ascent up from the dark, rich soil, the King's council would meet to decide the exact day for the celebration of their land being reborn. This time of year to us is just spring, but the tradition for these people to celebrate the earth "coming back from the dark winter" went back hundreds of years. They called this holiday "The Sun's Rebirth."

After the council had studied the land and the position of the moon and the stars, the exact date for the holiday was announced, and the townspeople immediately began planning for the big event. There were many different foods to cook, luscious breads and pastries to bake, houses to clean, and candles to make. The candles were very important because they were the people's favorite tradition. In each home, a candle was placed on every windowsill, and at the stroke of midnight, the candles would be lit. This would illuminate the whole town and be their way of saying "thank you" to the sun for shining strong once again.

Ever since the princess was a little girl, she had been responsible for the most important task for the celebration, and it was her favorite. She was allowed to place the candles throughout the castle windows and especially in the top window. When this, the top window's candle was lit, the town knew that the holiday officially had begun. For, by tradition, the townspeople couldn't begin to celebrate until the castle's top window candle was lit. They believed that this last candle revealed to the sun that they were ready for a new year of planting and harvesting.

The princess was getting excited that the holiday was fast approaching. She always had participated by helping her parents with the other preparations, but this year, she was a new bride and wanted to make the candles, bake the pastries, and do all the other tasks that needed to be done by herself. And, of course, she would be the one to light the candle in the uppermost window of the castle.

One morning as she was getting dressed, her lady-in-waiting rushed into her bedchamber. The council had announced the actual date. In just twelve days, The Sun's Rebirth holiday would begin at midnight! The princess was thrilled that she finally knew the exact date, but she also began to feel a huge burden of stress. Could she get everything done in time?

Sure enough, on the day that the candle lighting event would take place, the princess found herself in a mess! The candles still were hanging and dripping, not ready for the night's event. The store was out of sugar, and without sugar, she couldn't finish her baking. She also had forgotten to purchase matches, so she only had a few. Not to mention, the rooms of the castle that she had wanted to decorate with flowers and tree boughs weren't ready. How was she going to get all of this done in time for the great lighting? She fell on the floor in a heap, sobbing.

Soon, however, she felt a gentle hand on her shoulder. As she looked up through teary eyes, she saw her dear neighbor and friend.

"I have been in charge of The Sun's Rebirth celebration at my house for the last three years, and I thought that since this was your first year, maybe you could use some help," her friend said.

"I need too much help; I don't think anyone can help me!" the princess exclaimed in despair.

As her friend reached out a hand and lifted the princess to her feet, her friend laughed, pulled out a pen and paper, and began writing down what needed to be done.

The princess was amazed as everything started to come together. Her friend knew in what order things should be done: First, get the candles that were dry and see how many more they could add from her own extra candles. Next, go door to door, asking for extra sugar and extra baked goods that some smart villagers already had baked. And then send the town children into the valley to collect the new flowers and flowering tree boughs.

As the flowers and tree boughs were brought in, the princess and her friend began arranging them; though not in all of the rooms the princess had wanted. She soon began to cry about how small the decorations would be, but her friend gentle consoled her. She said, "Do what you can. The holiday is still wonderful whether one room is decorated or twenty are decorated."

Then, they started placing candles in each window, but only in those windows that could be seen from the town. That way they had just enough candles to place the last one in the high window.

Five minutes before midnight, the princess looked around and saw her table stacked high with wonderful food, windows full of beautiful candles, and the main room filled with the aroma and beautiful sights of flowers. She and her friend walked up the last few stairs to the top of the castle with plenty of time to spare. And just as she was about to light the candle, she handed the light to her friend. "I give you the honor of lighting the candle, for you made all of this possible," said the princess.

Her dear friend replied, "We did it together! So, let's light the candle together."

And they did. And so the town was all aglow with the warmth of thousands of lights, welcoming the rebirth of the land.

One of the morals of this story is that, even if we are princesses, without planning it is impossible to accomplish very much. My prayer is that you will be able to start planning your holidays so that you and your family will experience the joy that comes from these special times.

Without planning, it is impossible to accomplish very much.

Chapter 2

PLAN TRADITIONS AND MEMORIES

WHETHER MEMORIES ARE good, bad, everyday occurrences, momentous occasions, or one-time events, they are embodied in our thoughts throughout our whole lives. This is probably why mothers are so concerned with "building memories" for their children. While this is a good thing, we need to be careful that our intensity does not end up destroying our good intentions. Balance needs to be a part of our plans as we begin to form traditions and memories in our families. You might be able to relate to this story that I'd like to share with you.

❧ Balance needs to be a part of our plans as we begin to form traditions and memories in our families. ❧

Martha's annual Christmas party was a deeply set tradition and one she thought her mother looked forward to every year. However, as Martha was running around the city with her to-do list and arms full of packages, she was telling her best friend, Sandy, that if it weren't for her mother's love for the party, she would be tempted to reduce its size or skip the party all together.

Sandy was shocked. "But I thought you loved this tradition of throwing the annual Christmas party!" she exclaimed.

"Well this tradition has turned into an exhausting, expensive, and futile event that I don't even enjoy anymore!" cried Martha. "I don't have time for my husband or children, and yet I feel so guilty if I'm not fulfilling everyone's expectations, especially my mother's. I'd hate to disappoint her!"

Later that week, the day of the party finally arrived. Everyone was having a great time, although Martha's face seemed somewhat strained each time she tried to smile.

Halfway through the party, Sandy heard Martha's mother sighing in quiet desperation, "Why do I have to endure this party every year? I only come to please my daughter. She just lives for these parties."

Yes, Martha had fallen into the classic trap of trying to make others happy without finding out if they even wanted what she was planning. So, as I list tips for your holiday traditions and memories, please remember to ask your loved ones what they like best.

Making fond memories requires nothing more than embellishing daily routines in ways that reflect our values and passions. Meals, baths, story times, and bed times are all great opportunities to build meaningful rituals into daily life, while holidays and changing seasons may inspire those age-old, annual traditions.

Tips for Planning Traditions and Memories:

1. *Ask your family and loved ones what their favorite traditions and memories are.* Make sure you don't get defensive, make a face, or argue when they tell you! Be open minded, because the truth is, we want the energy we put out to bring the most happiness. I remember one Christmas, as I was getting ready to prepare for an activity that I had done for years, when my daughter said, "Oh, I don't really care about that, but I'd really love to . . . !" If she hadn't spoken up, I would have continued down an unnecessary path. Also, remember that it is especially important to talk with your husband about

Plan Traditions and Memories · 11

   what matters to him. It will show such respect and care for him if you want to know what he wants.
2. *As you begin to ask your family about their favorite traditions, write them down.* You may want to use some of the ideas one year and the rest another year. And make sure you keep some of their favorite decorations. Many times there is no need to stress yourself out by shopping for new decorations. Children love repetition and consistency, so a decoration that looks old to you may be their favorite one!
3. *Ask yourself what warms your heart the most.* For some of you, curling up in pajamas, watching movies, and sipping hot chocolate is a dream Christmas. Some of you want to spend hours in your kitchen. Follow your heart, and I believe you will create an atmosphere that will make everyone happy.
4. *Let each member of the family participate* in ways that use his or her skills and talents. Your little "drama queen" could put on a play, or your son could help stir the cake batter. Children love being a part of occasions and helping you.
5. *Make holiday happenings special by being there completely*—in mind, body, and spirit. Leave your paperwork at the office, and turn off your cell phone in honor of your family and the occasion. Your undivided attention is the most powerful memory-maker of all.
6. *Reflect on ways to be thankful all year.* Gratitude is one of the finest attributes we can have because it causes us to see all the positives in our lives instead of the negatives. It focuses our thoughts on the outside of ourselves rather than on the inside.
7. *Send out a family photo Christmas card.* This tradition is one of my personal favorites. Since I live in another city from where most of my adult life was spent, I want my friends to see how my children have grown. And I love to get picture cards myself. Make sure you start thinking of this picture in June. Why so early? Because sometimes it can be very hard to get everyone in a picture, and the summer vacation

shot works great. I used to have to send in the pictures for copies before Thanksgiving, but now many places can have your picture cards done in a day! (I use Costco.) My goal is to have the cards sent out by the first week of December.

Another option is to hold off taking the picture until Christmas Eve or Christmas morning. Then you will have a real Christmas picture to use! You could use one of the online photo processing services, such as Snapfish, Shutterfly, TinyPrints, VistaPrint, or Minted.com. On these, you easily can edit your digital photo, add a charming holiday border, and then order the number of prints you want. Some websites will even address, stamp, and mail the cards for you!

8. *Frame each Christmas family picture* and hang them all on one wall, or compile them in a small album. That way, as the years go by, you are able to see how each person has grown and changed.
9. *As you begin receiving cards, think of ways to showcase them.* I like to place them in a decorated basket after I have sorted them. A friend of mine places them on a string that is going up her staircase. The important thing is to have them out in the open so your family can enjoy them.
10. *Pray for the card givers.* I know of one family that prays for each family who sends a card to them. What a way to share the importance of prayer with your children!
11. *Write a Christmas letter.* If you decide to do this, make sure it is readable. The font should be large and the paper light in color—not dark red or green.
12. *Help others with their cards.* Prepare some cards for a relative or friend who is ill and unable to send cards out.
13. *Send cards for other holidays.* Remember that Christmas isn't the only time to send out cards. New Year's Day, Valentine's Day, Easter, and Thanksgiving are fine times for connecting with friends if Christmas is too busy to send out a card. One advantage in sending them out at a different time of year is that yours is one of the few and therefore extra special.

I have a friend in Denver who sends out a Valentine's Day letter each year. She drives to Loveland, Colorado, to get each envelope stamped with a special heart.

14. *Spend time baking.* Many people equate Christmas with baking. You can make and decorate a gingerbread house with your children. My daughters loved making one! And we were able to store it and use as a decoration for the next year. If this is something your family likes to do yearly, perhaps one year you could take the gingerbread house to a children's hospital or a neighbor. Another way to incorporate baking traditions is to bake homemade breads and desserts as gifts. Having one special baked good as your specialty that you give out each year is a tradition that serves as a memory to others as well as for your family.

15. *Check out community activities.* When we lived in Colorado, we used to love going to our community clubhouse on the first Friday of December. On that day, Santa was there for pictures, cookies were available to decorate, and they even had horse-drawn sleigh rides. I remember one particular Christmas when we were on the sleigh after a heavy snow. The moon was full, and it was gently snowing. This became a lifelong memory of a beautiful Christmas evening.

16. *Consider daytime activities.* If a daytime activity works better for your family, perhaps there is a place nearby where you can have "Breakfast with Santa." For those of you who would prefer not bringing "Santa" into your home, look for a special story time at your library or an afternoon tea with your older children. And, many churches need volunteers for their live Nativity scenes. What a great opportunity for a Christmas memory.

17. *Enjoy the lights.* One of my children's favorite traditions is driving around looking at all the Christmas lights. This can be as simple as driving down your own street, or it can last for hours! This also can be an opportunity to pray for your neighbors as you pass their houses.

18. *Start a scrapbook just for a particular holiday.* In a "Christmas Only" scrapbook, include all of the pictures, activities, and lists of gifts you received and gave so that they are all in one place.
19. *Go caroling.* If your children are in a group, such as scouting, choir, or a sports team, then you already have a ready-made group. This is a wonderful activity for the kids. It also is a gift to those who are unable to leave their homes—it allows them to be a part of the season.
20. *Go to a play.* Our family loved to see the ballet *The Nutcracker* each year. Many local schools and community theatres have seasonal productions that don't cost too much. This is a great way to support their efforts.
21. *Volunteer your time.* You can find a project that the whole family can be a part of: serving meals to those in need, delivering blankets to the homeless, helping in a food pantry or clothing closet, or "adopting" a family from your church or community and taking them food and presents. Many churches help you to do this easily by having an "Angel Tree" or other ways to help the needy.
22. *Enjoy the simple things.* Some of the best traditions are the simple ones. Set aside an annual night to relish simple, old-fashioned joys. Pop some popcorn and snuggle with a favorite book, or read one of your children's favorite stories to them. Watch a classic Christmas DVD, and then have a family sleepover in front of the Christmas tree.
23. *Have a party.* You can have a yearly party for your children and their friends that includes a night of games and pizza. You will be building memories for these friendships for years to come.
24. *Create a Blessing Bag or box.* A good friend shared this tradition with me, and I think it is an excellent idea: Place a wrapped box or special bag somewhere in the family room, in the kitchen, or by the tree. During the month of December (or November, if you want to do this for Thanksgiving),

have family members write kind and wonderful attributes and blessings about the other family members and secretly place them in the box. These can be anonymous or signed. Later, open the box or bag and read the comments out loud. Nothing is more uplifting or feels more loving than hearing and sharing kind words about each other!
25. *Take time to be outside.* Even if it is cold, you can take a walk through snow-covered woods, make snow angels with your children, and set up bird feeding stations. If you live in a warmer climate, grab a blanket, lie outside, and look at the stars. You can teach your children some of the different constellations as well as share the story of the Wise Men and their search for Jesus as they followed a star.
26. *Share the season with others.* Opening up one's home always has been a Christmas tradition in my family. When I was growing up, my mother had Christmas parties for each of her four daughters—at four different times on the same day! We would get the house ready, make all the treats, and then each of us would have our own open house party with our friends. This was so much easier than having parties on four different days. Then, when my children were growing up, we did the same thing. My younger daughter, Grace, had her party in the morning. I would have my annual Christmas Tea in the early afternoon. And then Christi would have her party late in the day. We have so many wonderful memories of cooking and getting ready for our parties together.

As I close this chapter, I'd like to share one tradition that has blessed thousands of people. In 1992, the Worcester Wreath Company of Maine had a problem. The selling season was drawing to a close, and Morrill Worcester had hundreds of unsold wreaths. What could he do? His mind went back to a trip to the nation's capital that he'd won as a twelve-year-old paper boy. Worcester had been deeply moved by his visit to Arlington National Cemetery. Now, years later, he loaded a truck with wreaths and received permission to decorate the graves at Arlington. That was almost twenty years and 75,000 wreaths ago, and the idea has since spread to other military cemeteries. Every year, hundreds of volunteers lay "Wreaths Across America."

Chapter 3

PLAN YOUR WORKLOAD AND DE-STRESS YOUR STRESS

I PERSONALLY FEEL that this is the most important step in having a more organized Christmas or family holiday. Since the goal of a more organized occasion is to give us more joy, more meaning, and (much) less stress, how we plan the required work is crucial for the holiday's success.

Steps 1 and 2 taught us to plan early and focus on the traditions and memories that are special to our families. Now we need a foundation to build on: planning for the *time* and *energy* everything will require.

There are some people who may remember a time when all that was needed to celebrate Christmas were a wreath on the door and a small tree. But as years went by, specialty stores opened, more and more ornaments, decorations, and events were added, and advertising increased to the point that now people may be quite overwhelmed with what Christmas has become.

Author and counselor, Elizabeth Skoglund, in her book *A Divine Blessing*, wrote this account of what happened to her tree decorating: "Christmas has always been a safety zone to me. I enjoy all the traditions and memories as well as the present friendships and meaning which I have connected with it. To me, one highlight is my Christmas tree. I have ornaments from my travels, ornaments from my childhood, and ornaments from cherished friends. And each year a few new ornaments seem to creep into my growing collection. I used to just have a pretty tree. But in the last few years that tree has become bigger and more elaborate, and people have begun to surprise me by making innocent remarks about my unique ornaments or how many ornaments there are. They ask other people, 'Have you ever seen her tree?'

"I used to always play Handel's *Messiah* while decorating the tree. That time was a safety zone every year of enjoying God and worshiping him through the words of that remarkable piece of music. But in the last couple of years, I have been too tired to worry about music while I'm doing my tree. Besides, it would take many renditions of that work before the tree would be decorated! I don't do it alone any more either; that too would take too long. I have ruined the wonderful tradition of decorating the Christmas tree by making the end product too elaborate. What was once a special tradition has become a chore, even something I dread . . . while the focus of decorating the tree is no longer my own personal satisfaction but impressing others."

I believe that what she has experienced is what happens to many of us during the Christmas season. We start out with such wonderful ideas and plans, but then they become chores and burdens rather than the special memories we would cherish. And our focus has been taken off of Christ.

So, how do we keep ourselves from getting overwhelmed and stressed the way Skoglund did? First, we need to remember that sometimes less is more. Next, we need to stop trying to "keep up with the Joneses" because we will not be able to. There always will be someone who has more than we have, just as there always will be those who have less. And then you need to think about how much time, energy, and effort you want to devote to the approaching holiday. As I said at the beginning of this chapter, it's time to build the foundation or the starting point for what you want to do.

> ❧ *You need to think about how much time, energy, and effort you want to devote to the approaching holiday.* ❧

Plan Your Workload and De-stress Your Stress

An easy way to do this is to first make a list of what you and your family have decided are the traditions and memories you want to pursue. Then, rate each activity with the amount of *energy* it will require by writing down a number next to it that is between one and ten—one meaning, "No! That is too expensive or difficult," up to ten, meaning, "Yes! I can't wait to do it!"

Remember that the energy necessary to create a holiday celebration depends less on brain or muscle power than on emotional enthusiasm. In other words, hard work is worth doing if you love it; but a task you loathe, even an easy one, qualifies as high energy. This is why it can be hard to decide what to do in a family group; every activity's score differs from person to person. One member may want to go to a tree farm and cut down the Christmas tree, and another person may dread it and only want a three-foot-high artificial tree! The next step, the *outcome* of the activity, will help with a compromise between these two desires.

After you have rated the activities, write down the *outcome* that the activities will have for you. A number one could mean, "I think that will be a waste of time," and a ten could mean, "That could be my favorite experience!"

Finally, multiply the numbers beside each activity and then rank the results from highest to lowest. Only keep doing the activities that rank the highest.

Holiday Decision Chart

Now, you can try making a chart so that you can see at a glance what is most important to everyone. Following the instructions above and using the example below, look at your to-do list and rate each task based on how much energy it will take to do the task and the outcome of doing it. Multiply the numbers, and then rank the results from highest to lowest. Remember, this will help you choose which activities your family wants to do and should help everyone have more of a voice in the decisions.

Christmas To Do List	Time/ Energy	x	Outcome/ Result	=	Payoff	Decision
Use real instead of artificial decorations	7	x	2	=	14	Use artificial
Build gingerbread house with kids	5	x	9	=	45	Do it!
		x		=		
		x		=		
		x		=		

After everything has been listed and rated, you can begin to see the payoff. *To have a happier holiday, simply give top priority to activities with the highest numbers!*

Do you remember the example I shared at the beginning of this chapter, about the tree decorating that became an unhappy chore? The author who wrote that probably would have put an eight in the Energy column and maybe a four in the Outcome column. The tree decorating had gotten out of hand, but she still loved the meaning of the different ornaments and how beautiful the tree became. A new strategy for her could be to have a tree-decorating party so she could get some help, and then find another activity she can do by herself as she listens to Handel's *Messiah.*

Be honest with how you truly feel about a particular event or tradition. If making the Thanksgiving dinner at your house gives you hives, even though you do it *every year and everyone is counting on you to continue,* it's time to make a change. Perhaps you could continue to host it but have everyone bring a dish. Or you could decide to change the location from your house to someone else's, or even to a restaurant. Look at the meaning and reality behind the work—things like being together with those we love—and not the food or the location.

Plan Your Workload and De-stress Your Stress

After your chart is finished, the next step is to write a plan of action. Begin your to-do list with the activities you have decided on from your chart. *Then, look at your master family calendar and begin plotting on the calendar:*

- When you plan on buying or making most of your presents.
- When you will get your tree and/or begin decorating.
- When you will wrap your presents.
- When you will get your house cleaned and ready.
- When you will cook and bake.
- When you will need to get time off from work.
- When you will be able to visit family and friends.
- When you will be with and play with your children.
- When you can help the needy.
- How you can make this season a special time with the Lord.

If the holiday you are planning isn't Christmas but Thanksgiving, Easter, or the 4th of July, the chart will work just the same. The focus on holiday planning should be on maximizing the joy and memories it will give yourself and others and minimizing the amount of stress.

And that leads us to the second part of this chapter: de-stress your stress! Stress is an unavoidable part of life, so we must learn to manage it. We also have to learn to manage stress so we do not become a perfect target for Satan and his many schemes. Remember, he "prowls about like a roaring lion, seeking someone to devour" (1 Pet. 5:8).

Stress can be caused by many things, including: sickness, loss of finances, a heavy work load, unending household tasks, raising children, unhappy family or friends, misplaced expectations, and perfectionism. If the thought of an upcoming holiday or your child's birthday party starts your heart pounding, then perhaps it's time to re-evaluate your priorities.

As mentioned previously, it's time to evaluate what is important and what isn't and then draw boundaries at the points that will keep you at peace. This is much more easily said than done because of all the expectations we place on ourselves, not to mention the expectations from others.

Perhaps understanding that stress can have a lasting effect on your health may help you make changes. According to a recent survey by the American Psychological Association, about forty-five percent of women experience heightened stress during the holidays while trying to juggle work and family demands. The survey cited lack of time, lack of money, and pressure to give gifts as primary sources of stress. This seasonal stress, in addition to high levels of year-round stress, can yield a lifetime of health problems, especially when women turn to food and alcohol to cope. We need to remember that our bodies are the temple of God! We are to keep this temple pure and healthy (1 Cor. 3:16–17).

Ways to deal with stress:

1. Learn your limits (physical and emotional) and set boundaries.
2. Take one day at a time.
3. Take needed breaks throughout the day.
4. Get enough rest. Go to bed on time. Wake up with a smile on your face and a prayer to God to start the day.
5. Have something to look forward to each day, week, and month.
6. Move your body daily. Stretch, walk, use exercise equipment, or do anything that will help your body to move. In fact, exercise is one of the biggest antidepressants there is.
7. Rest on the floor with a rolled-up towel under your neck for fifteen minutes.
8. Breathe deeply. "Just about every stress-relieving discipline involves deep breathing," says Dr. Mehmet Oz of New York Presbyterian Hospital. "It's an important foundation because it stimulates the brain stem and triggers the release of mood-modulating brain chemicals like endorphins and neuropeptides. Just a few seconds of deep breathing can

alter your brain's chemical balance enough to create a great sense of peace."[1]
9. Willfully remove negative thoughts and replace them with positive ones. "For as he thinks within himself, so he is" (Prov. 23:7). Your mind trusts what you tell it, so next time you are in a traffic jam, calmly tell yourself to be calm and that all things will work together for good (Romans 8:28).
10. Let prayer and meditation on God's Word be in your life every day, all day. Nothing is more powerful than prayer. "The effective prayer of a righteous man can accomplish much" (James 5:16).
11. Pray about *everything* (I Thess. 5:17).
12. Rethink what your expectations are. If they are too high, resentment can develop in your life.
13. Anticipating the inevitable need to forgive and pray for blessings on those people who offend you, let your holiday preparations include the emotional care of your own heart.
14. Make a list of everything you *have* done each day. Rather than getting upset with yourself for what you don't accomplish, get in the habit of celebrating your successes. That way, you will feel positive about how your day was spent, even if you weren't able to cross off everything on your list.
15. Pace yourself. Spread out big changes and difficult projects over time; don't lump the hard things all together.
16. Separate worries from concerns. If a situation is a concern, find out what God would have you do, and let go of the anxiety. If you can't do anything about a situation, forget it.

One aspect of stress that we don't often recognize is how it affects our children. Dr. Aditya Sharma, a child and adolescent psychiatrist, says his patients are usually more anxious during the holidays. That's because their parents are running themselves ragged with all they are trying to do and spending beyond their means for Christmas. Sharma says, "When you're telling your kids you're having a fantastic meal and lots of presents, but you're stressed out by an argument about how much money you've spent or how you're going to pay your next month's bills, or disagreeing with any of the plans, the kids pick up on that rather than what's coming out of your mouth."[2]

As many as forty-seven percent of tweens (defined as eight- to twelve-year-olds) and thirty-three percent of teens feel sad when their parents are stressed, according to a report by the American Psychological Association's "Stress in America" survey.[3] Sometimes parents, caught up in what they see as the "big" worries of holding on to a job, keeping a roof over the family's head, and putting food on the table, don't take kids' anxieties as seriously as they should, says Dr. Kay Allensworth, the Texas coordinator of the American Psychological Association's public education campaign. "It's that lack of perspective that leaves us surprised when kids commit suicide, turn to self-destructive behaviors or suffer poor health," she added. "We need to remember that parents can't help kids if they don't take care of themselves because their state of mind can often affect their children's state of mind."[4] Keeping our levels of stress low is very important.

One more way to reduce stress is this: don't compare yourself with others. It may look like they have it all together with their homemade cookies and ten decorated trees, but you never know if they paid someone to do it all or are overwhelmed with stress. Let me repeat: *you do not have to do everything.*

One of my friends only decorates with real boughs and real trees. She teases me about my artificial decorations, but that's all right with me because I like the ease they bring. I also might use slice and bake cookies rather than homemade because having some cookies is better than none!

It all goes back to what is important to you and your family and how you rate each activity according to the amount of effort it will take you in relation to the amount of outcome you want. Every day, we need to remember the true meaning for the season.

And for the other holidays in your life, staying low-key and having fun is way better than getting too stressed!

Chapter 4

PLAN YOUR FINANCES AND BUYING

WHEN WE WERE children, Christmas was the ultimate time to receive gifts. By the time we saw what Santa had brought, checked out the stockings, and opened all the presents, we were in gift heaven. However, most of our parents were in debt hell!

In the last fifty years, Christmas has become much more materialistic. The decorating and advertising begin before Halloween, and everywhere we turn, there is another advertisement convincing us to buy. And if we don't buy, we may begin to feel guilty. But Christmas is not about things. My hope is that this chapter will help us keep the proper perspective so that we can focus on what this holiday really is—a celebration of the best gift ever given, Jesus Christ—rather than on how many gifts we buy or how much money we spend.

❧ Christmas has become much more materialistic. ❦

If we think back to the first Christmas, we will discover that *God provided everything*! He decorated the stable with a star, planned the guest list (the angels and shepherds), sent gifts by way of the

Wise Men, and surrounded the young couple with two who already loved their son, Anna and Simeon, during baby Jesus' dedication to God. Mary and Joseph were so young and poor that they couldn't have celebrated this special birth in any other way than the way they did: receiving this gift freely from their God.

One aspect of Christmas that seems to be very important to us women is having our homes decorated, warm and inviting during this season. I couldn't imagine being homeless at this time of year. However, I read a story by a lady who had a financial situation that caused her and her family to have to move out of their house. I want to share part of her story with you:

> This past year our family encountered more financial hardship than ever before. We desperately sought God for answers and provision, and He provided both. While we listened for His answers, we believed He was telling us to rent our cozy home to in-training missionaries we knew needed an affordable place to live. We moved out of our house and into a one-room dwelling on our farm so they could move in.
>
> This wasn't our first choice for how God would provide. This provision included sacrifice and living differently than ever before. When our kids heard we were moving, the first thing they asked about was our annual family Christmas celebration.
>
> At first, I too was concerned we wouldn't have our home. But then I remembered Jesus left His home. He traded comfort for something that paled in comparison—all for a greater purpose.
>
> Jesus left the portals of glory, the very throne of God, the kingdom of Heaven, and the presence of His Father, to be born to a poor family in a common barn with animals. He wasn't born to just any poor family, but one of the weakest clans of Israel. There was no pomp or pageantry when He was born; He had nothing but strips of cloth to cover His body. Mary didn't get to order her favorite meal after the delivery or have the luxury of a comfortable bed to rest in that night.
>
> When they returned home, there were no balloons or people waiting to celebrate His birth. In fact, many in their small town thought Jesus was illegitimate. As a young man, He never acquired wealth or reputation. He even considered himself homeless,

with nowhere to lay His head. In His final days, He was rejected, mocked and tortured before being crucified. His entire life was one of sacrifice and obedience for His Father.

When I thought about everything Jesus sacrificed to come to earth, it made me embarrassed about my own expectations for a traditional Christmas. For so many years, I packed December so full I barely had time to reflect on the simplicity of the real story of Jesus' birth. It's a story of sacrifice and simplicity from beginning to end. Remembering the reality of Jesus' birth and His God-centered life assured me our move was God's provision.

The past few years have been hard. God has reminded me of a winepress. Repeated crushing is crucial to producing fine wine. Sometimes God allows us to go through repeated crushing to press us into His greater purpose.

This Christmas is different. We will set aside many traditions, such as a big decorated tree and gingerbread houses sitting in a row. Instead, we will celebrate Christmas more joyfully and humbly than ever before. We are learning that the hardest circumstances are often the things that push us into His greater purpose for our lives.

To celebrate Jesus' birth, we will go to the barn, scatter clean hay on the ground, read the Nativity story, eat a simple supper, and thank God for what He has taught us this year about provisions and sacrifice.

Next year, Lord willing, we will move back into our house. As a memorial to what the Lord has taught us, we will once again celebrate a simple Christmas, focused on Jesus' birth. Maybe we'll light a candle, read the prophecies of Jesus' birth, and study the Gospel account on the floor near a window. Maybe we will look out at the stars and sleep on the floor with a few provisions or comfort. Maybe we will eat crackers and drink grape juice together in remembrance of everything Jesus lived and died for.

May you and your family press into God this Christmas. May you experience His provisions and answers. Though His provisions might come with sacrifice, when you follow God's leading, they always bring you into His greater purpose. (From "A Simple Christmas" by Sharon Glasgow, www.sharonglasgow.com)[5]

This story really touched my heart and made me realize how easy it is to get more wrapped up in "doing" than "being" at Christmas. So I must ask this question: what must Jesus think of all this over-the-top commercialism? Would He be running through the store on Christmas Eve, trying to finish all of the gift buying and the last-minute decorations? Would He be charging on His credit card and not worrying about the debt that was adding up? I don't think so.

> *What must Jesus think of all this over-the-top commercialism?*

Since we want to have a more organized Christmas, as well as other holidays, let's now go to this next step of planning our finances and buying.

Planning our Finances

First, write down your financial goals and a budget. Don't worry! In case you have been reluctant to make a year-long budget, we are only going to take a small step and make a budget for Christmas.

Now, no one wants to be a Scrooge, but overspending can be hazardous to your finances as well as to your health and relationships. The majority of people in this country want to get out of debt, so if we work toward the goal of a debt-free Christmas, we will be on our way.

Ms. Gamoke, with Consumer Credit Counseling Services of Texas, said, "People feel so strongly about giving Christmas presents they fall down on their financial responsibilities. We also see people, instead of making their house payment, purchase Christmas gifts." *Twenty-three* percent of people won't be able to pay off their Christmas debt until March of the next year! If this doesn't strike you as stressful and in need of change, then think about if this is honoring the Lord or how He would want us to celebrate His birthday.

Now, let's begin by writing down the amount of money you have to spend on gifts and then list the people for whom you and your family need to buy. If there isn't any money for gifts (credit and debt don't count), then now would be a good time to call a family meeting about the upcoming holiday. This might be the year you bake or make your gifts, helping to keep yourselves out of debt. As hard as it will be for your children, they will learn a great lesson of saving for the future and doing without. There are many books and websites to help teens with money basics. One of my favorite is: www.daveramsey.com/school/home. He has information for elementary children all the way through college and also for the home-school child.

Another way to stay out of debt is to create traditions and events for your family rather than giving gifts. Or you can reduce the amount of gifts you give by only giving one gift per person, giving one present for a whole family, or making a holiday pact with your siblings or friends to keep presents at or under a certain price, such as $10.

You also could create a gift-pool, where you put all of the names in a basket and then each person draws one name to give a present. Remember not to use credit for these gifts. Our goal is to keep within the budget you have set, not to get in debt. If this is too hard for you, put the credit cards in the freezer to keep them out of sight! And be careful not to make any impulse purchases or succumb to sales or specials simply because they are "a good deal." Stick to your list of gifts you have planned to buy and get nothing else. Staying disciplined in your shopping is crucial to staying on the right track.

Of course, much of the debt problem at Christmas is a result of peoples' lack of planning before they go shopping, which is why a budget is so important. But other planning is important too. Consumer advisers suggest beginning Christmas planning in January. This means buying gifts throughout the year or saving money each month. Just $10 or $20 a week would amount to $500 to $600 to spend by December. Many consumers, however, often wait until Thanksgiving to start planning. That leads to shoppers rushing to stores with a vague idea of whom they need to buy for and what they need to buy, and they end up making impulse purchases that quickly add up.

As you are working on your budget, ask yourself if you are guilty of some of the money wasters on the following list. We all have at least some of them, but they can become a real blind spot when we are trying to stay within our budget:

1. Eating out too often
2. Spending too much on groceries, especially those items you never use
3. Buying just because something is on sale—do you really need it?
4. Spending too much on your children
5. Buying too many clothes or household items you don't really need

Remember that your budget is your friend, especially when January comes around. If you can stay within your budget, you won't have the stress of bills adding up later.

Now that you have worked on some of your spending blind spots, planned an amount of money to spend, and listed the people you will be buying a gift for, here are some tips on buying.

Plan Your Buying

Keep a log, either in your wallet or on a spreadsheet, of every gift you buy and for what person. You will be able to keep up with your gift buying better with a list, but also, you will be able to insure that you don't buy the same item for the same person in the future.

Buy throughout the year if possible. Have a special place in your home for these presents so you won't forget you bought them. Also, put the person's name and what the item is on the box. It is very easy to forget later what you bought. You may want another container just for stocking items so you can keep them in one place.

Set a date for when you want to be finished with all your buying. That way, you will stay out of the stores and out of debt! I try to be finished with all my gifts, wrapping, and shipping by the first of December. Then I can enjoy all the special things during the season.

Here's a good tip: you can recycle the Christmas cards that are extra meaningful or beautiful and use them as name tags for presents next year. Just cut off the front part of the card to use as your name tag, and then you can write on the back who the present is for and from.

Also, don't give money to children to buy gifts. This takes away the joy and sacrifice of giving. Children can make gifts or use their allowance money (or chore money) to buy gifts. Teach them to save all year for gifts. I still remember the gifts I gave to my grandparents that I was able to buy with my "own" money!

Here are some gift ideas that don't cost very much:

- Handwritten notes that share how you love and appreciate someone can be placed in a special keepsake box as a gift.
- Books are always great gifts for any age, but especially for children and teens to encourage their love for reading.
- Write a story for a special nephew or niece or grandchild with him or her as the main character.
- Record singing or speaking on a CD or tape a video of your family for those who live far away.
- Scrapbooks of special family memoires, reunion gatherings, a baby's birth, or a wedding can be prized gifts. These can be done by hand or online at websites such as:
    - http://www.scrapbook.com
    - http://www.creativememories.com

- Children love to put on shows, so they could perform a talent show or present a holiday recital as a gift.
- Create your own photo calendar by using extended family photos and then sending one to each family.
- If your family films are on video, put them all on DVDs as gifts for each family member.

- Let your Christmas card simply be your gift, if that helps you to stay in budget.
- Give personalized postage stamps with your loved one's new baby picture or new house, etc. Go to www.stamps.com.
- To help your children learn the joy of giving, look for some charitable organizations that your family could give a family gift to. One of my favorite charities is World Vision. Each year, they send out a catalogue with items you can buy instead of just giving money. My favorite gift item is a real baby lamb. Check out www.WorldVision.org. Another ministry for gifts is Samaritans Purse and Operation Christmas Child. They collect shoeboxes filled with needed items for children all around the world. You can visit them at www.samaritanspurse.org.
- Give your spouse (or child) the gift of time. Give them the "twelve *dates* of Christmas"! You could go ice skating, drive around to see lighted decorations, take a trip to get ice cream, give a back rub, etc.
- Gifts are not just for Christmas. When you are around the Thanksgiving table, ask each person to write a sentence or two about what is special about each person there. Then place these in envelopes to be opened later. What an encouragement it will be for each person to read the wonderful thoughts someone wrote about him or her!
- For parents of older children, put together all the scrapbooks, boxes of pictures, or awards your child accumulated throughout his or her life and present them as one large, organized box, book, or file. Your children will love the time you put into this project as well as the end result.
- Often the presents we shop so intently for are quickly forgotten. For a more memorable gift, I suggest doing something truly needed rather than buying something unwanted. Think about what you might do for your spouse, friend, or parent. Don't be afraid to ask what they really want. One friend, who knew her parents didn't like to cook, filled their freezer with homemade meals.

- Some families are interested in their ancestors. A great gift would be researching the family and presenting your findings to them in a meaningful way.
- Keep a basket of small gifts by the front door for carolers or anyone who comes to the house—a delivery man, mail person, neighbor, or child. These can be as simple as candy canes with a Bible verse attached to them.

To close, I want to share what one woman did to help her keep her sanity during the Christmas season. Author Ronna Snyder shared her heart in *Today's Christian Women* magazine:

> Peace became more elusive each holiday season. I'd lug out heavy boxes of ornaments to adorn my tree and home, trying to emulate the "perfect" Christmas look. Or spend hours in crowded malls, shopping for "perfect" gifts—items I knew were likely to be exchanged by their recipients. I'd toil over my family's traditional holiday recipes, convinced I'd be the world's worst mother if I didn't fix them.
>
> Then in a store, I suddenly thought, *"What must Jesus think of all this blatant commercialism?"*
>
> *That's it*, I thought. *I just can't "do" Christmas anymore.*
>
> Call it a holiday-mindset makeover, if you will. Hoping to put meaning back into a season that, for me, had lost so much of it, I decided to forgo nearly all our holiday traditions except great food and great times with family. I didn't put up a tree or decorations, didn't buy—or wrap—a single gift. Instead, I choreographed a Christmas my family pronounced "The best ever, Mom!"
>
> So, what did we do? We gave each other the best gift of all time. Stress-free, worry-free time. Not only times to contemplate the significance of Christ's coming to earth to save us, but time to actually "live it." Time to read, pray, think. And time to spend with each other.
>
> As a family, we made a list of fun and inexpensive local activities, and now, because we had the time, we did them. We bowled. We played pool. We went to the ocean. We ate out. We ate in (Costco did the cooking for us). And we finished it all off by savoring New Year's Eve fireworks displays. Together.

By stripping away the Christmas expectations I'd let bind me each year, we experienced every little bit of fun and spiritual significance the holiday provided—without the hassles and the guilt. Yes, I wrestled with the seeming sacrilege of having a nontraditional Christmas. But unwrapping Christmas freed my heart.

You may not want to follow this particular example, but I feel there are many women reading this who just might think it's a great idea. My prayer is that each Christmas celebration will be for and about Jesus Christ, sharing His love, and sharing His salvation with your family, as well as many others. And never forget that the first Christmas gift was God giving us His very own Son.

Chapter 5

Plan Your Decorating and Wrapping

I REMEMBER VISITING Rich's department store at Christmas time when I was a young girl. My siblings and I would get all dressed up in our Sunday best, drive to downtown Atlanta, and eat dinner in the Magnolia Room. Then we would go to the toy department, where Santa would be waiting to hear our many wants, and we would see a room stacked full with every toy imaginable. If we looked high enough, we could see the Pink Pig traveling on its little track throughout the toy store. Nothing was as important as riding the Pink Pig. I think that was even more exciting than seeing Santa! But what I remember most about these visits was how beautiful the store looked. There were so many Christmas trees, decorated with every type of ball or toy or satin ribbon or sparkles. Wreaths were placed on every wall, and the twinkling lights were everywhere.

As I got older, the city began having an annual event called "The Festival of Trees." Every type of tree and decoration was used to create an entire room, the size of a city block, with nothing but gorgeous and unbelievably decorated trees.

Perhaps as the professional decorators began to buy more decorations, people began to want to decorate more too. And when artificial trees started looking almost like real trees, then decorating for Christmas started becoming a year-long process. Instead of just buying Christmas decorations at Christmas time, you can find entire stores totally dedicated to this one holiday. Even the other holidays, such as Halloween, Thanksgiving, Valentine's, Easter, and the Fourth of July, now have their own decorations.

Nowadays, a family can have more than one tree and use different themes and colors. I heard of one family that has twenty-three Christmas trees! I don't know if I could handle that many, but it is fun to have different sizes and types throughout the house. Personally, I like to have one regular-sized tree in the foyer of my home, and then I have a small one in the family room and another small one upstairs, where the girls' bedrooms are. Each tree has a different theme and is decorated with different colors and items (more on this in a minute). And what is fun in today's creative climate is that nothing is right or wrong! You can have as many or as few trees or decorations as you want.

However, decorating your Christmas tree(s), as well as your home, is an undertaking of time and money. So in order to have a more organized Christmas, we must take time to plan this decorating.

> *In order to have a more organized Christmas, we must take time to plan this decorating.*

First, decide how much time, effort, and money you are willing to spend on decorating. *Second*, write down the theme, colors, and decorations you want to use. This will be your model or blueprint. For your theme, think about what you want to convey to your family and others during this Christmas season, or simply, what do you really like? Finding a theme will make the Christmas tree and home decorating so much easier because you will be able to focus on your theme and not become so overwhelmed by all the items and choices you see in the stores.

Many things can inspire a theme. For example, a favorite element from the Christmas story or a main color or a special type

Plan Your Decorating and Wrapping

of ball or decoration could be your inspiration for your tree and/or the house decorations. I love to collect angels, so some years ago, I decided that our main large tree would have angels and silver Christmas balls as its theme. I added gold and silver bows and long ribbons. I even have all the presents under the tree wrapped in the same gold and silver theme. Of course, the tree is never really finished. I add more angels and balls each year as I buy them or receive them as gifts. But I love the fact that I have a tree that now has become a tradition in our home. I don't have to start from scratch each year, and it just looks beautiful to me.

Since that tree is gold and silver, the small tree in the family room is done in the traditional colors of red and green. These ornaments are the most special and sentimental to me: pictures of the girls as children, ornaments they made, and some ornaments that were given to us. The tree upstairs is filled with the handmade ornaments the girls created over the years.

If you want to change your theme but the cost is too high to completely start over, think about just changing it gradually over the years. Add a few new ornaments, and give away a few old ornaments every year.

One option (which may seem like sacrilege to some of you) is not to have a Christmas tree at all. You just may not have the money or even the room for a large tree. Or you can't find the time or the energy to put up a tree. Please remember that if you are unable to have a tree this year, it is quite all right. The reason for the season is Jesus, not a tree! He wants to be received warmly into every home with love, time, and honor. And remember, there wasn't a Christmas tree at His birth. Instead of a tree, find or make simple decorations for your table or mantel.

Or, if you simply can't imagine Christmas without a tree, find a tiny tree. My grandmother had the sweetest, porcelain tree that was probably only about 12–18 inches high. She would wrap white angel hair around the bottom and set the tree on top of her television set. I loved that tree and all the simplicity it represented.

Third, find a time on your calendar when the whole family is free to go out and find a tree or to get it out of storage. I will say that the best organization tip for Christmas is this: have an artificial tree that is already pre-lit. I save hours because I am able to take our tree out of storage, pull the protective bag off, and presto, the Christmas tree is up and ready! Yes, my mother thinks it's awful not to have a real tree, but the time and energy I save is enormous. I love to have my house decorated; I just don't want it to take very long. (Note: be sure the tree is labeled as fire resistant.)

Once you have your tree, designate a time so the family (or those who want to be there) can be a part of decorating the tree. I know that children can make a mess of your pre-planned perfection, but memories and their attachment to their family is worth it! Put some classic Christmas music on and perhaps set out some treats, such as eggnog, hot chocolate, or cookies. Be sure to let each child participate: the older ones can help with the lights, and the younger ones can help decorate the lower branches. Even a toddler can help take a decoration from you and hand it to someone at the tree. You may even want to start a tradition where each child has a favorite ornament that only they hang on the tree.

For those who are new at decorating a Christmas tree, there really is no right way to do it. For trees without the pre-strung lights, David Stark, a Brooklyn, New York, floral designer, shared a trick to hanging lights on your tree: go up and down, not around. Start by dividing the tree vertically into three sections and string the lights by sections. Always plug in the lights before you begin, to identify any defective bulbs. Start at the bottom, and weave each string in and out of the branches, going to the top of the tree and back. This process helps to create an inner glow of light, along with a three-dimensionality that cannot be achieved any other way.

Fourth, find time on your calendar to decorate the rest of the house. I usually can't decorate the same day I do our tree because of lack of time or energy. Make a list of what you want for the mantel, the dining room table, the kitchen nook, the powder room, and the front door. Please remember that you don't have to decorate everything I just mentioned! But these are some of the more common places where your family and guests would enjoy seeing decorations.

Keep in mind that you can make many of your decorations by using items you already have. As an example, if you like candles, walk through your house, collect all the candles you aren't using, and place them in the center of a table or on the mantel. You can then weave natural boughs of holly or tree clippings to cover up any of the candle holders that don't match. If your budget allows you to purchase more candles, find some that are the same color but different heights and widths. They can really make a beautiful statement for your home. Another idea is to start buying battery-operated candles. They are made of wax and come in several shapes and sizes. Instead of a flame, they have a flickering light that is placed deep into the center and operates with a switch on the bottom. I love these because I get worried about a candle burning up too quickly and either melting on a good table or even starting a fire. (Check out www.batteryoperatedcandles.net.)

Another way you can decorate cost-free is by finding natural items outside. Take a family walk and collect pinecones or large acorns to decorate your Thanksgiving table, or spray-paint them gold or silver or red or green for a Christmas decoration. If you have a magnolia tree, cut off some of the flowers and greenery and place them in a large bowl. The smell and its beauty are heavenly. You can even put some of the magnolia branches in your unused fireplace to decorate it. Also, link bunches of greenery with colorful ropes and tassels that follow your theme. These can be placed on your mantel, a long table, or even on your staircase. If you live by the ocean, shells make beautiful and unique decorations. They can be glued on a wreath or made into tree ornaments.

I love pulling out some of my clear flower vases and containers and filling them with balls of one color and with holiday lights. Or you can fill these containers with candy: candy corn for Thanksgiving, jelly beans for Easter, and candy canes for Christmas. Add a ribbon, flower, or some greenery and you have a special and new decoration!

Styrofoam balls wrapped in ribbon make beautiful tree ornaments or decorations for your home. You also can add greenery or fruit or tiny glass Christmas balls to a Styrofoam circle for a wreath.

When you make things yourself, you can stay in your budget, besides being able to stick with your personal style and likes.

My favorite chapter in my cookbook is "Kids Can Cook Too!" I think it is important to let our children be a part of the holidays as well as everyday life. So include some decorations that they can make for your home—inside and outside. Children like to help decorate. My children liked to make outdoor "bird feeders" that also served as decorations. To do this, first allow some bread to harden. Then cut out pieces of the bread with cookie cutter shapes, cover them with peanut butter, and sprinkle the pieces with bird seed. You can hang these on a wire or hooks (coffee cup hooks work great) on trees. Or children can string fresh cranberries and hang them on your Christmas tree, the mantel, or on tree branches outside.

And of course, nothing is more fun or traditional than making Christmas cookies. But besides making cookies, children also can make dough "ornaments" that look like cookies but are used as ornaments! There is a recipe for this at the end of the chapter.

The next step in organizing your home for the holidays is to make your home look welcoming. I know for many women, entertaining can be very difficult and outside their comfort level. But don't despair; here are some tips that can help you accomplish this quickly and beautifully!

First, focus on first impressions. I know you think the sofa is old and the rug is frayed, but I promise, people really don't notice those things. What they do notice are the front door and the foyer of the house. Take a pen and some paper and go to your front door and outside stoop, as a guest would, and write down what you could do quickly to make a nice first impression. Do you need to sweep the front steps or rake some leaves? Are there any cobwebs around the doorbell or in the corners of the door or porch? You may want to sweep or shake out the doormat—or, if you can afford one, purchase a new doormat. Check the light bulbs and see if any need to be replaced, along with cleaning or dusting the light fixture.

Second, look around and think about what would be a quick way to decorate this area. My favorite is a wreath on the door. I have a different one for each season of the year, and it looks like a "welcome sign" on the door to me! Perhaps you could place some flower pots in a corner and fill them with the different seasons' flowers, such as tree boughs at Christmas or brightly colored mums for Thanksgiving. You even could pile in assorted pumpkins, gourds, fall leaves, and a bale of hay. I also have seen large holiday figures that can be placed right by the front door—wooden Easter bunnies, Santas, reindeer, nutcrackers, scarecrows, etc.

Now, walk inside your home and see if you need to freshen up and clean the foyer. Make sure you check out the hall closet. Pull out anything that doesn't belong there, and place some extra hangers in there (nice and strong ones) for your guests' coats. If you don't have room for any more coats in the closet, then either remove some of yours temporarily or have your guests place their coats in a bedroom. Or you could rent a coat rack. If you live where it snows a good bit, you may want to place a small rug for your guests' boots or wet shoes by the front door. It's also nice to have an umbrella stand close by. In addition, be prepared with shovels and/or liquid de-icer (such as Icenator), salt, or kitty litter for your walkways and driveway.

Next, see if you could add a decorative touch to this area. If you have a table in the foyer, then just a small vase with flowers or a holiday decoration is plenty. If you are having a party and will need name tags, this is where you will want to place them, along with a pen. If you don't have a table, set up a temporary one. It helps guests to feel more at home if they already have their name tag on before they begin to meet the other guests. Plan to have someone—it can be you or someone else—in charge of this area to greet the guests, take their coats and/or pocketbooks, and help them with their name tags.

Now is also the time to look over the room where you will be entertaining. Rearrange the chairs so that you have a large seating area where everyone can talk freely. If some of your guests will be watching TV for the football games or parades, be sensitive and keep that section of the room quiet. If you don't have enough chairs for everyone, borrow some before your guests arrive. They will feel very welcome when they come into your home and see that you have already made your home ready for them. A simple appetizer on the coffee table and a corner of the room set up with children's toys are other great ways to make your home welcoming.

Remember that you don't have to make your home perfect for guests. If we did, I don't think we ever would have them! So skip the heavy cleanup and focus on where the guests will be. The guest bathroom can be made ready with just a spray cleaner and some paper towels. Clean the countertop, sink, and mirror, and then with the used paper towels, you can wipe the floor quickly. Empty the trash can, add fresh toilet paper (even if there is ½ roll left, you won't worry if you start with a new roll), clean the toilet, put out some clean hand towels, make sure you have enough liquid soap or new soap bars, light a scented candle, and you are finished!

Next, make sure your kitchen looks clean by cleaning the countertops and sink. When you are cooking all day for your guests, this can be hard, but your food will look much more appetizing if the kitchen looks clean. Try to keep the dirty dishes moving into the dishwasher or a sink filled with soapy water and as much order throughout the kitchen as you can. If the sink isn't big enough, fill a large, plastic bin with warm, soapy water. As the dishes get used, place them in the bin until you have time to wash them or add them to the dishwasher. You also can light a candle in the kitchen that smells of gingerbread or apple pie. Remember, our goal is not perfection but a welcoming atmosphere.

An hour or two before people start arriving, turn down the thermostat a couple of degrees so that they (and you!) won't overheat once everyone's packed in and the oven is in high gear. You also can crack a window open to circulate fresh, cool air, and then adjust as the party heats up.

Turn off your bright overheads and use amber votive holders, which give off a warm glow. These votive holders can be placed on the edges of steps, down the center of a table, or on end tables.

Once you get your home to look welcoming, you will be able to breeze through these steps much more quickly, even when you have those spur-of-the-moment drop-ins. I promise, you will have many fond memories if you are able to enjoy having friends and family visit in your home.

Wrapping

Part of decorating your home for Christmas is wrapping the presents that will go under your tree and those that will be sent off to your friends and family. I think the most important tip in wrapping is to designate a place (a command center) where you can wrap throughout the season. It could be a room, a card table, or a corner of your kitchen. But having a central location will help you keep it all together: scissors, tape, gift tags, pens, etc. If you have the budget, purchase a weighted tape dispenser (so you can get a piece of tape one-handed) and nice scissors. They even sell a special type of device that can cut wrapping paper in one push.

Make a list of each person and the gift(s) they are getting so you can cross them off after you have wrapped the gift(s). Make sure you label the gifts immediately, or you may forget whose presents they are. Gift tags can be bought or, as mentioned earlier, made from last year's Christmas cards. I also wrap different families' presents with wrapping paper assigned for each family so that I don't get them mixed up when shipping or delivering them.

As for the paper you use, shop around and look for the color and style you prefer. You may even want to make your own wrapping paper. Martha Stewart shows people how to do this, but personally, I don't want all that work torn up in seconds on Christmas morning! I also look for good bargains on wrapping paper. If a roll only has a few feet on it, it probably is too expensive. I like the large, thick rolls of paper because they last longer. If cost is an issue, you could use brown bags and decorate them, or even use the Sunday comics!

Storing wrapping supplies is also important. I use a large, rectangular, plastic bin for all of my supplies so that my ribbon, gift tags, and paper are stored together. I keep my ribbon in a small box so it doesn't get tangled. But you can store your ribbon on a paper towel holder for easy access. A hanging toiletry bag also makes a perfect trimmings tool kit, since the clear compartments mean your equipment stays accessible and visible, and it can hang (or get tucked away) when not in use. If you have a lot of different rolls of paper, store them in a clean trash bin that can be stowed away after the season. So papers don't unravel and rip, slip thin rubber bands (the thick ones can grab and rumple paper) around the tubes. Also, you can store non-seasonal wrapping paper in the same trash can to help keep all your wrapping paper together.

When the Christmas season is over and you begin to pack up your decorations, take notes on what you will need next year and buy it in January. You may not feel like buying Christmas supplies, but prices can drop by seventy-five percent, and it's so nice to open your wrapping bin the next year and have it already stocked and ready for the season!

Let me give you one last suggestion. As I mentioned earlier, I do believe that at times, less is more. One or two beautifully wrapped presents show more care than a load of hastily wrapped ones. When someone really takes the time to buy me a present he or she knows I want or would like and then gives it to me with beautiful tissue or wrapping paper, it does show love and caring. I have been guilty of just trying to get the wrapping finished without thinking about what I was doing: putting together a gift to show my love.

Yes, all good things come to an end, and so does a holiday. This is the part I dislike the most: *packing up the decorations*. But it must be done, and I highly recommend that you set up a system that works best for you.

When I am taking down decorations, I like to go from room to room, picking up everything and taking it to one place, usually my dining room table. That way, I can clean those rooms, place the furniture back, and be finished with those rooms of the house. Then I pack everything away in plastic bins, each one labeled with exactly what is inside for easy locating next year. (Since everything is corralled in one central place, I can take my time at this step, since the rest of my house is back to normal). If anything is broken, now is the time to either fix it or throw it away. I also write down anything I may need for next year so I can get it in January, while it is on sale, or so I won't forget next year. In addition, it's a good idea to write down notes about your decorating: what worked, where you put items, what you need to replace, and what you want to add next year. Make sure you take some pictures of what you did so you can repeat it.

This is also the time to clean your ornaments. You actually can remove the dust from them with a blow dryer on the lowest setting and then cushion them with sheets of paper towels, white tissue paper, plastic grocery bags, or fabric softener sheets when packing them up for the year. Don't wrap your ornaments in newspaper; the ink can smudge onto them.

If plastic bins are too expensive to purchase for storage, liquor-store boxes are wonderful. They are already divided up into sections, which are great for storing your ornaments. You then can tape a Christmas card on the outside of each box so you know what holiday it is for, and make sure you label it well.

Here are a few other storage ideas:

- Empty egg cartons are great for tiny trinkets.
- Empty paper towel tubes work well for garlands.
- You can wind a string of lights around the packaging it came in. However, if this has been thrown away, you can use empty coffee cans. Cut an "X" in the plastic top, and stick the plug through. Label each string with masking tape and mark which lights go on the inside tree and which ones go outside.
- Old hosiery can protect specialty candles from getting damaged. Slip knee-highs over the pillars to keep them dust free. Then nestle them in tissue paper to prevent dents or scratches, and stow them away from heat or pressure, which can melt or warp the wax.
- Treat wreaths with the same care you would your clothes. Slip the hoop over the neck of a coat hanger and then cover the wreath with a plastic dry cleaning bag to prevent dust from building up. Hang wreaths in a closet or from a beam in your attic.

These tips can be used for the other holidays you may decorate for too. The best preventative thing you can do is to take the time to store your decorations carefully and correctly. Opening a box of broken or dirty ornaments can take away holiday cheer fast! Don't be afraid to ask for help in putting away decorations and delegating. You can't do everything. If your family members were able to enjoy the holiday, they can help put it all away!

Do-It-Yourself Christmas Decorations Dough

(From *12 Steps to Becoming a More Organized Cook* by Lane P. Jordan)

2 cups all-purpose flour
1 cup salt
1 cup water
Food coloring, if desired

1. Combine flour and salt in a large, flat-bottomed bowl, and then very slowly stir in the water a little at a time, until a ball is formed. You can add food coloring at this time for a marbled effect or add food coloring to the water for an even color throughout.
2. Knead the dough for 7–10 minutes, until dough has a smooth, firm consistency. Add a little water if needed.
3. Place dough in a plastic bag to prevent drying. Then it may be stored in the refrigerator for up to five days. (*Remember, dough sculptures are art, not food. They are not edible!*)

- When making decorations, bring the dough to room temperature.
- Use foil-covered cookie sheets for a work surface and for baking.
- Flour your hands and work surfaces to keep dough from sticking.
- Roll out dough to about ¼ inch thick.
- Cut ornament shapes out of dough with cookie cutters.

- With a toothpick or nail, make a small hole at the top of each ornament so you can hang them with a thread or ribbon.
- To add your own decorative touches, form small pieces of dough and attach them with water.
- You may air dry the ornaments for forty-eight hours, until they are very hard. Or you may bake them on their foil-covered cookie sheets at 325 degrees until they are golden brown. This takes around thirty minutes. But make sure you watch them through the oven window. Thin pieces bake more rapidly, are more likely to burn, and may need less time.
- Fill any cracks with moistened dough, and let the ornaments air dry.
- Allow them to cool and then decorate them.
- You may then draw a design with white glue and sprinkle it with glitter, sequins, buttons, seeds, bells, etc. Or you can paint the pieces with watercolors, acrylics, enamels, or spray paints.
- Your ornaments are now ready to give as gifts or hang on your tree!

Chapter 6

PLAN YOUR MEALS

I DON'T THINK a holiday could be a holiday without food! So organizing and planning all the food is very important. For me, this is the hardest part of any holiday. I love the decorating, getting the house clean and ready, and all the parties. But the meals still have to be planned and the extra cooking has to be done in an already busy schedule. This is why we have to get organized.

❧ *I don't think a holiday could be a holiday without food!* ☙

The first thing to do when planning for holiday cooking is to sit down with your calendar and write down how many times you will want to bake or cook and the events you will do it for. This will take a lot of communication with your husband, family members, and friends. You also will need to ask yourself questions such as: Will I bake items for gifts? Will I make meals for the needy? Which meals (Thanksgiving, Christmas Eve, Christmas, Easter, etc.) will be at my house? Will I need to make my annual Easter bunny cake for the grandchildren, or are they too old for that tradition? Will we eat out in a restaurant this year? Will I bring in food already prepared, such as a turkey, from a restaurant or grocery store?

Once you have settled on *when* you will be cooking, it's time to plan *what* you will be cooking. Look over your recipes and plan the menus and the corresponding shopping lists. Christmas and other holidays are *not* the time to experiment with new recipes! Cook meals you are familiar with, and you will not have as much stress. And cook recipes that you can have multiple dinners from to give you more time during this season. Also, think about the types of snacks you want around the house for company, including friends or family who may drop by. One tip that may help is to have the ingredients for a favorite appetizer already in your pantry or freezer so you quickly can prepare a tasty appetizer in a tight pinch.

Make room in the refrigerator, freezer, and pantry for the extra food you will need to store. This is the time to clean out your refrigerator and discard everything that's past its prime! At least one month before Christmas, begin your baking. Most baked goods freeze nicely. If you find a recipe that everyone loves and you enjoy baking, make it easy for yourself and bake it every year. Repeated traditions are so much easier! Remember to do your holiday grocery shopping one week before the holiday, since stores do run out of popular items. And cook as much as you can ahead of time.

If you are going to do a lot of baking for gifts, then decide what types of wrapping you will need to buy. If you make a loaf of sweet bread, you may want a festive bag. If you like to make cookies, you may want a plastic tray or plate that the recipient can keep.

The Holiday Dinner

If you are the one hosting the holiday dinner, don't panic! God calls us to be hospitable, and I promise that with some of these tips, the meal and the event will be a wonderful time for you and your family.

First, decide what you want to have for the meal. Look through your recipes and begin to make the menu. I would use tried and true recipes that you are familiar with. Then, decide which items you would like to delegate. Usually, the host prepares the meat (turkey or roast) and some appetizers, and the other guests bring the salad, starch, vegetables, and desserts. I have done an entire dinner myself, but it really is more fun and so much easier to have everyone bring a dish.

Next, determine how many people will be attending and if your dining table is big enough. If not, set up some bridge tables. If you don't have any, ask to borrow extra tables and chairs from a neighbor or family member. Get these set up two or three days before the event. Yes, that may sound early, but the way to keep you from panicking is doing everything early! Once the tables are set up, you can begin to set the tables; sometimes this takes longer than one would think. That's because holiday linens are usually boxed away in an attic or closet, and we tend to forget exactly what we have for each occasion and if they need ironing or mending.

One year, I had more people for dinner than usual and realized I was lacking one charger. I quickly sent my husband out, and fortunately, he found a box of four that matched mine. If I hadn't started setting the tables early, I wouldn't have had the time to locate a missing piece. Now, I know the world won't come to an end if we don't have all the pieces to set our tables, but if we want to have a peaceful and more organized holiday, this helps.

After you have the table linens or mats on the tables, get out the china, glasses, and flatware, and then set the table(s). Remember, if you don't have enough plates, that's fine; the plates don't have to match. People just want something to eat off of. Then begin deciding on a color theme and centerpiece, unless you have one that you use each year. Remember, it doesn't take much to make a beautiful table. Some foliage and candles work beautifully. One note: if you freeze candles for at least a couple of hours, it will keep the wax from dripping.

I love Spode's Christmas Tree china pattern, so over the years, I have been collecting pieces of it. I love to use it for the whole month of December. But if you want one type of china to use for all the holidays, I suggest white. I have found some of the most beautiful white china, a full set of ten or twelve, already boxed for a great, inexpensive price. White china can be used for every holiday.

All you need to do is change the color scheme of your table linens and decorations.

After the tables are set, get out all of the serving pieces you will need: casserole dishes, platters, bread baskets, butter dishes, meat trays, and all of the utensils. Place these where you will set up the buffet, or if you aren't using a buffet, set them on the dining table. Inside each dish, place a sticky note that says what item it will hold. Place the appropriate large spoon, slotted spoon, meat fork, butter knife, etc. by each dish. Now you can get a clear look at everything that it is on the menu and where it will go. And you won't be in a panic at the last minute. I even have a sticky note set out for a dish someone is bringing. That way, I won't forget it is coming, and I'll have space on my buffet table for it.

One nice touch is to label all of the dishes at a meal so that everyone knows exactly what they are and if they can eat them. If your sticky notes are neat and legible, you can place them right in front of the dishes. Or you could use special cards, such as place cards, for this purpose. It is especially important to label the coffee as regular or decaffeinated and the creams (half and half, a flavored creamer, etc.).

You also may want to set up an area for drinks. Instead of setting these up in your kitchen, set up a small table (such as a TV tray table) with an ice bucket, glasses, and napkins. This will give you a central place for drinks without people stepping on you in the kitchen. Be sensitive to what your guests like to drink. If you know they can't drink anything with caffeine, plan an alternative. Keep a pitcher of ice water out at all times. You also can make a punch. This is an easy drink to prepare so you don't have to have ten different types of colas around. And remember the little ones. If they still are using sippy cups, place these out for them. If you are serving hot chocolate, for fun, you can use candy canes as spoons. It is also a good idea to put someone in charge of the coffee machine to keep up with filling the sugar and cream and making a fresh pot of coffee as soon as it is empty.

If you are serving buffet style, place butter, salt, and pepper on the buffet table and also on the dining table(s). Condiments need to be accessible. Also keep backup supplies close by. Catering pros will tell you that napkins, utensils, and glasses always get dropped or lost in the meal's bustle. Don't feel you have to have a fancy buffet table to set out a buffet! I have a center island in my kitchen that I use for buffets all the time, no matter how formal the occasion. I feel it is much easier for a guest to choose what he or she wants and the amount rather than passing heavy dishes around a table.

With so many items to cook for a holiday meal, a 200-degree oven works as a warming drawer. This frees up counter space and provides insurance that your food won't burn if you forget to take it out.

Over the years, I have heard many wonderful traditions involving the Christmas meal. One is to set a place of honor for Jesus at your Christmas dinner table as a reminder of His presence. (He is the reason for this wonderful season.) Another is to seat couples together. Usually at a restaurant, they are seated across from each other. Party books will tell you to split couples up, but I think couples need to sit by each other so they can share and talk during a holiday meal. Yet another tradition is the use of place cards so you can maximize the seating. These can be handmade and reused as the years go by or given to the name holder as a gift. Along with the place card, there could be a question to answer, such as, "What do you remember from past Christmases?" or for Thanksgiving, the classic question, "What are you thankful for?" These are wonderful ice breakers as well as a great way for our children to learn more about their relatives' lives.

What do you remember from past Christmases?

Another tradition is reading the Christmas story when the meal is over. This is also a perfect time to pray for each person and ask for a blessed New Year. If you have young children, a fun tradition is making a birthday cake for Jesus. Let them do as much of the cake as possible, and then they can present it to the guests at the

Christmas meal. It brings the true reason of Christmas home to them, and it helps them to feel a part of such a busy time.

Cleanup Made Simpler

I believe one reason more women don't want to have an elaborate holiday meal is all the cleanup time required. I hope some of these tips will help the cleanup process go much more easily so you will be more inclined to have people over:

First, don't be afraid to ask for help! Most guests want to help, and especially during a holiday meal, they want to be a part of the occasion. You need to delegate as much of the meal and details as you can. However, some people may be offended if they are asked to help clean, so this is where understanding how your guests may want to help is important.

Next, clean as you go. As soon as you are finished with a pot, pan, bowl, or utensil, place it in the sink and get a helper to start washing it or place it in the dishwasher. (I prefer washing all of the large pieces by hand to make more room in the dishwasher.) And make sure the dishwasher is empty before dinner begins. Once the clean items are dry, place them in the laundry room (or another unused space) until you can put them away later, or if you have time, tell someone where they go in your kitchen.

After the meal, fill up your sink or a large, plastic bin or ice chest with hot, soapy water. Then as the plates are brought into the kitchen from the eating area, scrape them in a ready trash can (this is faster than using the sink and the disposal), and place them in the soapy water until you or a helper can wash them. Note: it is very helpful to line the broiling or roasting pans with foil before using them so that baked-on bits, grease, and drippings are easily tossed away. It is also important to wipe up spills as soon as they happen.

If you don't want any dishes to clean, buy paper products that are quite colorful and make a beautiful table. If you are using paper products, make sure you have plenty of empty trash cans ready for them. Note: double or triple line the trash can so you already have a clean bag in place when a full bag is removed.

Assign certain helpers to pack up any leftovers, and pre-arrange which storage containers they can use by having them, along with foil and clear wrap, already out and on a counter. Ask your helpers to label each container. If you know ahead of time that you are going to want to send some leftovers with your guests, buy some inexpensive storage containers that they can keep.

Ask one or two other volunteers to be in charge of clearing the table and explain how you want the table linens or mats handled. Usually, you can just go outside and shake them and then place them in the laundry room until you have time to spot treat and wash them. If you have a great helper, she could do this for you and place them in the washing machine to soak overnight.

Remember: it doesn't have to be perfect. If you only have a limited time with your guests, then get the cleanup to a certain point and then stop and enjoy your guests. Ask your husband and children to help you later. As long as the table is cleared, the food is put away, and the dishes are soaking, most of the work is done! And if the weather is very cold outside, you simply can cover and place many of the dishes outside on a screened porch until you have time to get them ready for the refrigerator.

Breaking bread with others has been and always will be one of the most important traditions we have. In fact, Jesus' last time with His disciples was when they had Passover supper together. My prayer is that as you prepare a holiday meal for your family and friends, joy and love will be the main ingredients.

May God bless you and all your Christmas and holiday meals.

Chapter 7

PLAN TIME FOR FAMILY, FRIENDS, NEIGHBORS, AND THE NEEDY

CHRISTMAS AND OTHER holidays are known to be times of peace, joy, and good tidings. We see commercials and movies showing families nestled around their fireplaces with hot chocolate, excitedly anticipating the surprises yet in store for them, while the glitter and sparkle of the season light up their eyes.

One would think that the holidays would be the best times of the year. But sometimes that isn't the case, and it's mainly because of the deep-seated, often unspoken problems we have with our family members. The new daughter-in-law doesn't understand her new family's traditions, and so she feels left out and different. Mom is mad at her teenager for a thousand reasons. The teenager is also angry at Mom, especially because she has to dress up for the family dinner. And the little ones are just too tired and antsy to sit still for the family photo.

If you think you have problems with your family, just think of this young family at the first Christmas: Mom and Dad's fourteen-year-old daughter is pregnant. However, she claims she is a virgin and that an angel told her the daddy is God. What would you do if your daughter came to you with this type of story? Can you imagine the shock, the crying, and the confusion? No wonder this young teen was sent away to her cousin Elizabeth's house while her parents figured out what to do. And what makes the story even worse is that this young girl was engaged to be married, but the fiancé knew he wasn't the father. The law commanded that he have her stoned to death. What should he do?

Yes, the couple in this story is Mary and Joseph, but we've all read the story so many times that it's easy to forget that these were real people with real problems, just like us.

Family dynamics can be complicated. Each person has his or her own expectations and agendas, and when you combine these with a holiday full of stress in close quarters, you can get an unhappy occasion. It seems that nothing is more irritating than a family member getting on our nerves. Still, while we don't get to choose our relatives, we are called to treat them with respect, love, and honor—regardless of how we feel about them.

But how can we do this? Read Romans 12:18: "If possible, so far as it depends on you, be at peace with all men." That, however, can be pretty difficult when the "Griswolds" or some fussy relatives are coming to visit! We must seek God's guidance through His Word, where pivotal examples equip us to deal with difficult relationships.

❧ Family dynamics can be complicated. ❧

Some family challenges revealed in Scripture include these examples concerning . . .

Parents and children:

Noah's son Ham embarrassed him, while his two sons Shem and Japheth protected his honor.
—Gen. 9:18–27

Jacob tricked his father, Isaac, to receive a blessing.
—Gen. 27:1–40

The new widow, Ruth, chose to stay with her mother-in-law, Naomi.
—Ruth 1:16–18

PLAN TIME FOR FAMILY, FRIENDS, NEIGHBORS, AND THE NEEDY

Siblings:

Cain killed Abel over approval of sacrifice.
—Gen. 4:1–12

Esau sold his birthright to Jacob for a meal.
—Gen. 25:29–34

Later, Jacob stole the blessing that his brother, Esau, should have received from their father, Isaac.
—Gen. 27:21–29

Joseph was rejected by his brothers and sold into slavery (Gen. 37:12–36), yet he chose to forgive them.
—Gen. 45:1–28

Marriage Issues:

Abraham pretended that his wife was his sister.
—Gen. 12:11–20; 20:2–7

After trying to have an affair with Joseph, Potiphar's wife lied to her husband about the incident.
—Gen. 39:6–23

Ananias and Sapphira cooperated together in lies and deceit.
—Acts 5:1–10

Even Jesus faced challenges within the family structure. His mother, brothers, and sisters were disturbed by the crowd's persistence and attempted to pull the Lord away from His followers. They did not understand Him and said that Jesus had "lost His senses."[6]
—Mark 3:20–21, from *In Touch* magazine, 2009

These biblical examples helped me to realize that no family is perfect and that no matter how hard we try, there will be times of family discord. Think about the difficulties you currently are dealing with in your family. In what ways can you commit to showing compassion and patience in those situations? Whom do you find hardest to love in your family? Commit to praying for those individuals and asking the Lord to provide opportunities to grow in your relationship with them. Before any family get-together, make sure you pray, asking the Lord to give you His wisdom, power to love, and patience so that you, as His child, will be a good example.

It often has helped me to pray for God to love that person through me. I already know I cannot do it by myself. But God can! And He can turn an uncomfortable group setting into something that will glorify Him. He also can give you the strength to create a new you in the old family setting. For some reason, our nature seems to fall back into how we acted with our family members many years ago when we were immature and perhaps not walking with the Lord. So, prepare your mind and heart to forget past injustices. Show honor to your parents and love to your siblings in obedience to the Lord.

Here are a few more tips that may help:

1. *Create boundaries.* If one family member has embarrassed or hurt you in the past, perhaps you need to contact that person before the family occasion and share how he or she hurt you. If that person continues his or her bad behavior when you do get together, just walk away. If there is someone who really knows how to set you off, keep away from him or her. (Note: if you have been the victim of sexual or hurtful abuse, you need to talk with a professional Christian counselor about any contact you should have with your abuser.)
2. *Let go of expectations.* Expectations about what other family members should or shouldn't do can be a source of great conflict. It's unfair to assume that your in-laws think and believe as you do regarding family time, food, entertainment, etc. Heartache and disappointment occur when we expect others to act or be a certain way. This is so important to recognize because I believe most of our family problems come from the expectations we place on others.

Jesus taught us to "lend, expecting nothing in return" (Luke 6:35). When you have family around, your time, energy, resources, and support need to be given out of a spirit of love—with no strings attached. This will encourage everyone to relax and enjoy one another just as they are.

3. *Think before giving advice.* This is a hard one, but remembering this can make such a difference! Yes, you are right that too much dessert will only make your brother's diabetes worse, but this is Christmas or Thanksgiving dinner. Let it go. Many times a suggestion or opinion, when not invited, can become a sore spot between family members. Unsolicited advice about a daughter-in-law's weight or a brother's spending habits only encourages resentment, strife, and defensiveness. I love these verses in the Bible: "a man of understanding keeps silent" and "a prudent man conceals knowledge, but the heart of fools proclaims folly" (Prov. 11:12; 12:23). And James 1:19 exhorts us to "be quick to hear, slow to speak and slow to anger." Before we share advice, we should ask ourselves first if this is advice worthy of sharing.

4. *Remember that others have different ideas.* Not everyone in a family will be like-minded. Disagreements about such topics as politics, religion, child rearing, education, hobbies, and cultural interests can lead to misunderstandings and contention. Your opinion is really only important to you! Even if you make all your own baby food and your sister buys hers from the store, allow her to run her life the way she wants to. You never know if others will change their choices when they see the positive outcomes from your choices, without a single word ever coming from you.

And remember that you don't want to alienate family members! By loving them, you will be able to experience some wonderful memories that won't happen if there is conflict. "And be kind to one another, tender-hearted, forgiving each other, just as God in Christ also has forgiven you" (Eph. 4:32).

5. *Speak in truth and in love.* I think this is the hardest thing to do in a family setting because I don't want others to be angry with me or not to like me. But sometimes we need to speak out. For example, if their kids are tracking in dirt, or the car is being borrowed without their adding gas, or no one is going to the store except the host, then you need to share your specific needs, boundaries, or frustrations. Many times, when we openly share what is bothering us, we find that others aren't even aware and are more than happy to change.

    Family members also may have certain needs or habits that you need to take into consideration. As my parents began getting older, it was easier for them to stay in a hotel rather than in my home or my siblings' homes. It didn't mean they loved us less. It just was easier for them to keep their own schedule in their own place. And we needed to understand that. Perhaps some of your family members drink too much. If so, then don't serve drinks when you are hosting at your house. Will they get mad? Probably. But it's your house, and you get to set the rules.

    The important thing is to let all of your decisions be based on God's love. Scripture calls us to love with the agape love that only the Holy Spirit can fully make a reality in us. In the love chapter of 1 Corinthians 13, the apostle Paul explains that this kind of love shows patience, kindness, and a desire to trust. Love isn't jealous, boastful, arrogant, rude, selfish, or easily angered, and it doesn't harbor a list of grievances.

6. *Remember to pray.* I don't know how anyone can make it through a day without prayer to the Father. I need His help, His wisdom, and His strength for everything that goes on in my life. If you are in a difficult family situation around a holiday, pray that God will help you through it. Pray that God will give you love for that family member and will give you the right words and the grace to make the occasion a beautiful time for all involved.

While being together may be uncomfortable at times and you may need to bring up issues that should have been dealt with long ago, the Holy Spirit always is available to help us "walk in a manner worthy of the Lord" (Col.1:10). Remember to apply His Word to your actions and attitudes so that this "happy, fun family time" will turn into a special holiday gathering full of love, memories, and a new love that will bind you all together.

7. *Don't forget your marriage.* With all the comings and goings during the holidays, it's easy to let our most important relationship slide. I know you are busy, but nothing is more important than spending time with your spouse. If your marriage is doing well, the rest of the family will be more at peace, and all the holiday gatherings will be much more fun and go much more smoothly. So plan time for each other; remember to say, "Thank you"; be financially responsible by communicating and being a good steward of the household funds; take time to kiss goodbye and hello, hold hands, or give a quick touch on your spouse's shoulder as he or she walks by; make sure each of you takes time for yourself; make sure neither one of you overextends yourself; and let the small things that irritate you roll off your shoulders—after all, there are so many other things to dwell on. Relationships, and especially marriages, take effort, work, and time, even during the holidays.

This purpose of this chapter is to reflect about the people we have around us at Christmas. Family, of course, is the most important group we spend time with around the holidays. But another important group is our friends. In fact, some friends are family to us when we don't have any family members living near us. Since we pick our friends, the times we spend with them are special indeed. Inviting them for dinner and other activities can bring wonderful memories. I encourage fostering these relationships because they can add so much to your life. Jesus had twelve friends He spent every day with for three years. We all need friends in our lives.

> ❧ *Some friends are family to us when we don't have any family members living near us.* ❦

A third group of people to remember at Christmas is our neighbors. When my daughters were babies, I started having a Christmas tea for all the neighbors in my neighborhood. I felt that this was a perfect way to reach out to them, those neighbors I didn't know as well as a way to share the Gospel message during the Christmas season. I continued the tradition as we moved from Georgia to Indiana and then to Colorado and lastly to Texas, my current location. The girls loved to help me with these parties, and as they got older, they would have their own parties on the same day, just at a different time, as I previously mentioned. We would plan the food together, bake together, and help each other with our parties. We always would read the Christmas story during the children's parties, and I prayed that there would be seeds of faith planted in those little hearts. I loved doing our parties every year. You may feel the same way and want to start a holiday party yourself to get to know your neighbors.

Other ideas of things you could do with the children in your neighborhood are:

- Gather them together and go caroling in the neighborhood—what a wonderful way to witness as well as to bring joy to the children!
- Invite them to your church's Christmas service.
- Have some neighbors over to bake.
- Make cookies, do a cookie exchange, make gingerbread houses, or make reindeer food. (Blend Cheerios, oatmeal, glitter, and sugar; place it in a small gift bag; and have the children sprinkle the "food" on the lawn on Christmas Eve.)
- Have a gift-wrapping party so everyone can come over and wrap their gifts together.

There's another group of people I want to discuss: the needy. The needy in your life may be a neighbor just down the street who

Plan Time for Family, Friends, Neighbors, and the Needy

has had a baby or surgery and needs a hot meal, babysitting, or her house cleaned. They also could be the brave young men and women in our armed forces.

Here are some ideas of how to help those in need:

- Consider "adopting" a soldier from www.anysoldier.com.
- Consider adopting a "twin family." That's a family that has the same makeup as yours (single, married with no children, single mother with two children, etc.). Call your church or local social services department for contacts and shopping guidance.
- Instead of exchanging gifts with your girlfriends or coworkers, contact the director of a local women's shelter or a pregnancy care center and get a list of items you can purchase to help them. You could have a party to package the gifts in baskets and all go together to deliver them.
- Remember the senior citizen centers and nursing homes. They do get a lot of visitors during the Christmas season, so perhaps you can visit them in July for a "Christmas in July."
- Offer to take homebound neighbors or the elderly shopping.
- Call or visit anyone you think might be alone or who has lost a loved one during the past year.
- Go through your children's toys, and let them choose toys to give to the needy.
- Help single mothers with errands, babysitting, and meals.
- Volunteer at a local food bank or soup kitchen, especially during Thanksgiving, when the need is so great.
- Donate your eyeglasses, clothes, and household items. We have so much, and many people have countless needs.
- Here are some websites that may give you more ideas: www.seniorcorps.gov; www.americorps.org; www.1-800-volunteer.org.

Remember that the reasons we are on this earth are to live for Christ and do for others. Doing a little bit of good wherever you are really is doing a lot! If people are hurting or alone during the

Christmas season, let them know you care, that you are there for them, and that you are praying for them. "Let your light shine before men in such a way that they may see your good works, and glorify your Father who is in heaven" (Matt. 5:16).

Chapter 8

PLAN TIME FOR YOURSELF

LAST WEEK I was having lunch with a dear friend, and she asked me what writing project I was working on.

"I'm working on how to have a more organized Christmas," I said.

And then, without missing a beat, she came right out and said, "I hate Christmas."

She caught me so off guard that I started to laugh and said, "Sometimes, I do, too!"

Now, don't start writing me letters. But what we meant in these statements is that Christmas is *hard*. You probably will understand by the time you reach the age my friend and I are (our children are grown and out of the house). We have done just about everything a mother can do to make sure our children have the best and most special memories of the Christmases they experienced throughout their childhood. Now our bones creak as we put up the tree, our memories fail as we start to buy presents, and at times, having twenty-five people over for dinner is more confusing than joyful.

"I think I'm going to suggest to my husband that we should take a trip this Christmas," she decided with glee. "Then I won't have to decorate at all!"

12 Steps to Having a More Organized Christmas and Holiday Season

Now, I know what you are thinking. Lane, if you dislike Christmas, why are you writing a book about it? Because, dear friend, I *love* what Christmas represents! *But I am so frustrated with what it has become.* It seems that each year, more and more of us try to outdo everyone else with our inside as well as our outside Christmas lights and decorations. We feel that we must attend every function, musical, play, and party. So by the time it's all over, most women in American are exhausted, depleted, and beginning to dread having to do it all over again next year.

> *Most women in American are exhausted, depleted, and beginning to dread having to do it all over again next year.*

Now, at this stage of my life, I can become overwhelmed with just opening all of the Christmas storage boxes! It seems to take days rather than hours to decorate the house, and that doesn't include decorating the outside of the house. What is even harder for me is packing it all back up! Sometimes, I do get discouraged and exhausted. I also realized I hadn't done anything for myself in the time between Thanksgiving and New Year's Eve.

One summer day, I was up in the attic and saw all those boxes full of Christmas decorations, and the first thought that went into my head was, *Oh, no, only six more months before I have to do all that again!* It was then I realized I needed to find a way to be more organized at Christmas so I wouldn't lose the beauty and the magic and the true spiritual reason we celebrate in the first place.

Some of you reading this book understand exactly what I am saying. But I'm sure there are others of you who are more like my mom. She just loves Christmas and will spend hours upon hours decorating. Her home really does look like the December cover of *Southern Living*, and I love being in her home at Christmas.

Whichever type of woman you are, you still need to take time for yourself. And taking time for ourselves during the busiest time of the year takes planning. That's what this chapter is all about. I want you to really enjoy this Christmas! I want it to be full of joy and love for you. But for that to happen, you will have to make some changes.

Survival Tips and Stress Reducers

Below, I have listed some tips to help you take care of yourself during the Christmas season:

- Get enough sleep. Specialists say that the best present you can give yourself this year is the gift of sleep. Try going to bed at the same time each night, and then during the day, take time to just sit and rest for a few minutes.
- Keep expectations reasonable. Don't take on more activities than you can handle comfortably. It's all right to say "no" to projects that won't fit into your time schedule or that will compromise your family or your mental or emotional health.
- Take one day at a time. Tomorrow will take care of itself. (Matt. 6:34)
- Take deep breaths throughout the day.
- Pace yourself. Spread out big projects over time. Don't do too much at once.
- Listen more and talk less. (James 1:19)
- Act like an adult, but play like a kid!
- Laugh as much as you can every day. It truly is medicine for the soul. (Prov. 17:22) And remember to laugh at yourself.
- Develop a forgiving attitude; most people are doing the best they can. (Col. 3:13)
- Develop a thankful attitude; be grateful every day, all day, for at least five things. (I Thess. 5:18)
- Focus deeply on each moment of each day.
- Stop at times during the day and take a long look outside: at the sky, the clouds, the flowers, and the trees that God has created.
- Turn off the TV and radio more often.
- Use your cell phone less and try not to use it around your children.

- Be kind to everyone, even to those who are unkind. They need it. (Eph. 4:32)
- If someone is mean to you, don't retaliate. Never do an evil for an evil. (Rom. 12:17-20)
- Try to stay as organized as you can, for that will reduce stress. Keep important items, such as car keys and wallets, in the same place. And have extras: an extra car key in your wallet, an extra house key buried in the garden, extra postage stamps, extra bread in the freezer, etc.
- As mentioned in the chapter on finances, don't overspend. Plan a holiday budget and live within it, regardless of the temptations. Financial burdens can cause more stress than almost anything in a marriage and family. You may want to buy presents all through the year to keep from overspending.
- Do not run up credit-card debt. Perhaps this year you can make or bake your presents. Begin an experiment of going days without spending money on anything other than basics.
- Learn to shop online, if that would reduce the temptation of buying.
- Be careful how you eat. You are the temple of God. Focus on what you are eating at every meal and every snack, and purpose to eat healthily. Eat a healthy snack before going to a party to diminish your appetite. You may also want to make a pact with your husband or a friend to be accountability partners together to help each other eat appropriately. (I Cor. 3:16)
- For those of you who drink, be careful of your alcohol intake. This, of course, is for your health, but it also allows you to give more of the real "you" when you are with family and friends.
- Take along your own healthy dish to a potluck get-together and, if possible, to a holiday dinner.
- Save calories by drinking water!
- Understand that children can experience stress during this time. Slow down your schedule for them; take more time during meal times; be available to talk; and be sure to communicate what's going on each day.

- Get up and going each day. Make sure you keep up on your chores. Be sure you move your body by doing vigorous chores, exercising, or taking a walk. Exercise produces natural stress reducers.
- Be patient with an annoying person. (Gal. 5: 22-26)
- Lose any grudges you may have. (Heb. 12: 14-15)
- Don't obsess so much. Not everything can be perfect.
- Don't complain. If you have to, write your complaints down and put them in the trash! (Phil. 2: 14-16)
- Let it go. You will have loss and difficulties throughout your whole life. Give it all to God in prayer so that you won't have to worry or be upset. (Phil. 4: 6-7)
- Reach out to someone who needs comfort.
- Get outside for at least a few minutes each day and feel the sunshine on your face.
- Drink water throughout the day. Dehydration causes fatigue, which can affect your mood.
- Smile, even when you don't feel like it.
- Do something special for yourself every day, even if it's just sitting down with a cup of hot tea.
- Don't try to control so much. The greater your need to micromanage things, the more stressed you're going to be. Jesus said, "Take my yoke upon you, and learn from Me, for I am gentle and humble in heart; and you shall find rest for your souls" (Matt. 11: 29-30). Let Him be in control.
- Pray; read God's Word, the Bible; and find time to be alone with God, every day. (Mark 1:35)

I know you probably have heard these stress-reducing tips before. But I also know that you probably have a hard time doing them. So maybe this next section will be the motivation you need. You see, when we apply some of these tips to our lives, we actually are able to *slow the aging process*!

Dean Ornish, M.D., of the Preventive Medicine Research Institute in Sausalito, CA, led a group of scientists in a pilot study of men who had been following a healthy lifestyle of exercising for half an hour each day; eating a diet rich in fruits, vegetables, and whole grains, along with foods low in fat and refined sugar; and spending an hour a day taking part in stress-reducing activities, such as yoga or meditation. As expected, the men lost weight, lowered their blood pressure, and increased the activity of disease-preventing genes.

But something else happened that was even more exciting: The healthy lifestyle spurred a twenty-nine percent boost in the activity of an age-defying enzyme (called telomerase) that usually declines with advancing years or disease. Nothing else, no drug, has ever been able to make this enzyme work as well in helping with our cellular aging. The potential life-extending benefits are for everyone. "Your body's cells are aging, but there are lifestyle changes you can make to slow down the process," says coauthor Jue Lin, Ph.D., a molecular biologist at the University of California, San Francisco.

Anything that can help stop my body from aging is something I'm interested in! So taking care of ourselves with the food we eat, the exercise we do, and the rest/prayer time this study mentioned should be at the top of our to do list, even during the busy Christmas season.

Beyond diet and exercise, there is also another way to help us stop aging, and that's through our thoughts, beliefs, and behavior. "There's good evidence that emotional, spiritual, and social factors are all important for longevity," says Gary Small, M.D., director of the Center on Aging at UCLA. Research shows that these four strategies help the most:

1. *Be positive and outgoing.* People who have a positive outlook when they're young end up living longer. Even when a person is fifty, just feeling upbeat about getting older is linked, on average, to seven more years of life, research at Yale University has found. "Negative emotions like hostility and bitterness are bad for overall health and specifically for the heart," says Stephen Post, Ph.D., director of the Center for Medical Humanities, Compassionate Care, and Bioethics at Stony Brook University in New York.

2. *Do good for others.* People who volunteer at two or more organizations have a *forty-four percent lower death rate than those who don't do any charitable work,* the Buck Institute for Age Research in Novato, CA, reports. "That's comparable to exercising four times a week," Post points out. Like working out, helping others seems to boost antibodies. "We're establishing biology of compassion involving the immune system, brain, and hormones," says Post.
3. *Remember to pray.* A University of Texas survey showed that when we regularly attend a house of worship, it may slow our progress towards death by seven to fourteen years! But attendance is only part of the picture; it's the underlying belief system that provides comfort and improves health, says Duke Researcher Harold G. Koenig, M.D. In other words, when we stop our busyness to focus on our Lord, pray, and meditate on His Word, we become healthier.
4. *Have positive relationships in your life.* People with strong social connections enjoy better health, and this translates into longer life. "The support of solid relationships boosts immune function," says Dr. Small. And marriage may be the most important relationship. Studies show that married people live longer, say researchers from the University of Chicago. People who have strong social ties age well and tend to cope with aging more easily. Our obedience to God's command to "love one another" could be one means through which He blesses us with good health![7]

I hope as you are reading this chapter, you are beginning to understand how important it is to plan time for yourself. Realize that when you are healthy and rested, you truly will be able to enjoy all that goes on with these wonderful holidays.

Christmas After a Loss

During this time that is normally full of joy and festivities, we need to understand that there's another dimension of Christmas that can cause stress and sadness. At some point in your life, you or a loved one will face the holidays after a time of grief and loss. When that happens, be aware that your feelings will come unexpectedly, triggered by Christmas carols, family traditions, or holiday smells. There's an intense sadness and unbearable loneliness when we are missing loved ones. Their places at the table are vacant, their laughter is heard only in our memories, and we long for the touch of their hands or the sound of their voices.

For those of you who are experiencing your first Christmas without a loved one, I want to say that I share your pain and understand how violent the feelings of loss and loneliness can be. Rick Warren, author of *The Purpose Driven Life*, said that loneliness is the most common pain people suffer. This pain intensifies at Thanksgiving and Christmas.

Here are some tips to help you get through this difficult time:

1. Focus on following God's plan for your life. He is in control.
2. Reach out to other people and their hurts and needs. This will help take your thoughts off of yourself and onto others.
3. Realize that God's presence is in your life. Stay in His Word daily.
4. Give yourself time to cry and to get in touch with your grief.
5. It's OK to break traditions. You may need the change during this time of grief and transition.
6. If the empty chair at the table is too difficult to see, then either set a place of honor for your loved one or remove the chair all together.
7. Decorate the way you want: very little or over the top. Either way is right if it helps you to cope with your loss at this time.
8. Have the phone number of a trusted friend, counselor, or pastor close by in case you start to get very sad or depressed.
9. Every day and every moment of your life, realize that you can choose either joy or sorrow.
10. Live in the present, and look for things that, even amid the grief, can be moments of delight.

As mentioned above, doing for others can ease our feelings of loneliness and sadness greatly when we have lost a loved one. The story below shows how a wonderful tradition came from helping others.

The History of the Candy Cane

We aren't sure if this story is true or not, but this is how the story goes: About two hundred-thirty years ago at the Cologne Cathedral, the children that went to church there were really loud and noisy. They often moved around and would not pay attention to the choirmaster.

This was very difficult for the choirmaster because he needed the children to sit still during the long, living Nativity ceremony. So to keep the children quiet, he gave them a long, white, sugar candy stick. He bent it on the end to look like a cane. It was meant to look like a shepherd's cane, and so it reminded the children of the shepherds at Jesus' birth.

In 1847, a German-Swedish immigrant in Wooster, Ohio, put candy canes on his Christmas tree, and soon others were doing the same. Sometime around 1900, candy canes came to look more like what we know them as today with the red stripes and peppermint flavoring.

Some people say the white color represents the purity of Jesus Christ and the red stripes are for the wounds he suffered. They also sometimes say that the peppermint flavoring represents the hyssop herb used for purifying and spoken of in the Bible. The shape also looks like the letter "J" for Jesus, not just a shepherd's cane. It is possible that these things were added for religious symbols, but there is no evidence that is true.

Around 1920, a man in Georgia named Bob McCormack wanted to make candy canes for his family and friends, to help them feel the Christmas spirit. He later started mass-producing candy canes for his own business, which he named Bob's Candies. This is where many of our candy canes come from today. (Copyrighted by MyMerryChristmas.com. Used with permission.)[8]

Chapter 9

PLAN TIME FOR THE GUEST OF HONOR

I LOVE SPECIAL occasions. I love getting dressed up, going to fun places, and giving and receiving gifts. When we have these fun times in our lives, our lives have a higher level of satisfaction and joy. These events pull us out of the ordinary rut of living and give us new excitement and delight. For any of you who ever have had time in a hospital or been on bed rest at home, you probably know the excitement and fun you feel when you get out of your "prison" and start to enjoy life again.

Well, our Father in heaven loves to have fun too! In fact, He is an event planner! God created and planned festivals for His chosen people. Throughout the Old Testament, God commanded the children of Israel to observe these holy days to celebrate life, to better understand what He had for their future, and to serve as memorials to the mighty things He had done in their lives. There were nine major holidays and Sabbath days instituted by God in the Old Testament. Seven of these were appointed feasts, meant to be a sacred time when the Israelites met with God. Three of these seven appointed feasts were pilgrimage feasts, when all Israelite males were required to appear before the Lord at the temple in Jerusalem. These Old Testament feasts and holidays, according to

Paul in Colossians 2:16–17, were a shadow of the things to come through Jesus Christ.

The feasts and holidays include the:

- Passover (Pesach)
- Feast of Unleavened Bread (Hag HaMatzot)
- Feast of Firstfruits (Yom HaBikkurim)
- Feast of Weeks or Pentecost (Shavuot)
- Feast of Trumpets or Rosh Hashanah (New Year)
- Day of Atonement or Yom Kippur
- Feast of Tabernacles or Sukkot (Feast of Booths)
- Rejoicing in the Law or Torah (Simchat)
- Feast of Dedication or Hanukkah (Hanukkah or Feast of Lights)
- Feast of Lots or Purim

> *God created and planned festivals for His chosen people . . . to celebrate life.*

Since Jesus was one of the children of Israel (aka Jewish), He celebrated these feasts and holidays each year. You may remember the story when Jesus, as a twelve-year-old boy, was accidently left behind in Jerusalem. His family and friends had gone into the city for one of these feasts, the Passover (Luke 2:41–52).

Now, I don't want your eyes to glaze over with this history lesson, but there is a reason for my sharing this with you. If we understand what God has done in the past, we may get a better understanding of what He wants us to do in the present. I believe He wants us to continue to honor His Son with feasts and celebrations. That is what Christmas and Easter are all about. My prayer is that we honor His Son with our hearts and souls and spirits and not with a perfectionist, pressured plan in which everything is perfect but we are miserable. That is why I wrote this book: so we can organize our lives and plans in such a way that our holidays are *centered on Him*. Then God is honored and our lives are rich and full with His presence.

God said, "These are my appointed feasts . . ." In Leviticus 23, God even gave detailed directions. God told Moses to make an announcement, inviting the entire nation. He said, "Rejoice, come together, drink and eat, sing, praise, rest from regular work, bring gifts, breathe the pleasing aroma, and celebrate." How wonderful to know that God loves celebrations and must be thrilled when we celebrate His Son's birth!

We can organize our lives and plans in such a way that our holidays are centered on Him.

So, what are some ways you can honor Jesus at His birthday celebration? As you read some of the ideas I have, write in some thoughts you have about things you and your family could begin to do.

Ways we can honor Jesus, the Guest of Honor, at our Christmas celebrations:

1. *Let the focus of your home be on Him.* Perhaps the central point of your decorations could be the nativity scene. Or the decorations on your tree and mantel could be items that reflect the Lord and His Kingdom.
2. *Have a "Happy Birthday, Jesus" party.* This could be for your children and their friends, your own friends, or just with your family. You could have it before Christmas, Christmas Eve, or on Christmas day. (As I mentioned in another chapter, baking a cake for His birthday is a wonderful activity to do with your children, and it allows them to be a part of celebrating Jesus' birthday.)
3. *Set up a Menorah.* Yes, a Menorah is part of the Jewish holiday, Hanukkah. But Jesus celebrated with one during His lifetime! I got one for my daughters, to teach them where their faith originated from. Children love lighting the candles each night, and I believe it helps to bridge the gap between the customs of when Jesus was a child and ours today.

4. *Get an Advent Tree or Advent decoration.* We had an Advent kit that included a tiny Christmas tree and twenty-five small, numbered boxes with an item in each box. A book came with the kit, and so each day, we would read that day's devotion and then open the box that corresponded to that day. It was such a blessing to take time to focus on Christmas and what the birth of Christ means.
5. *Read a Bible verse each day.* Again, the wonderful part of doing this is that we stay focused on Christ and allow this celebration to be all about Him.
6. *Make a Blessing Bag.* A friend gave me this idea. You hang a decorated bag either with the Christmas stockings or at a focal point in your house. Or, if you prefer, you could decorate a box and set it in a prominent place. Each person in the family writes on a piece of paper the blessings God has given them that year and places it in the bag or box. You may do this once or as many times as you wish. On Christmas day, the bag is opened and the blessings read out loud, reminding us of the blessings given to us by our Father in heaven!
7. *Take time each night to read wonderful Christmas stories and books to your children.* We love books, and so throughout the years, we started collecting many Christmas books. Each December when we unpacked our decorations, we would find all of our Christmas books and keep them displayed around the small tree by the children's rooms. Each night, my daughters would select a book to read. What a great way to find quality time for your children during this busy time of year, as well as to focus on Christmas.
8. *Read out loud to your children Luke 2, which is the real story of Christ's birth.*
9. *Take time to listen to beautiful Christmas music.* I keep my Christmas CDs separate from the rest of my CDs so I won't have to hunt for them each Christmas. We start playing them Thanksgiving weekend as we begin to decorate the tree. I believe music is a beautiful way to connect to our emotions,

others, and the Lord. I highly recommend that you find time to listen to some this next Christmas. It will calm your spirit and give you a peaceful feeling. It's a wonderful way to take care of *you*.
10. *Offer Jesus Yourself: mind, body, and soul.* Give Him an area of your life that you desire to change, such as an emotion, an activity, an addiction, or a relationship. Write your commitment on a piece of paper, place it in a box, and wrap it as a Christmas present. You could open the gift on Christmas day and share with your family the change you are giving to Christ for His birthday, or you could place the wrapped present in a personal area of your home so that only you and He know what is in it. Either way, giving our whole self to Him is the greatest gift we could give the Lord!

Although we celebrate Christmas on December 25, no one knows the exact day when Jesus was born. His birth may have been in autumn, when the weather was still warm enough for shepherds to be outdoors with their flocks. We do know that Jesus was crucified on Passover and that the Holy Spirit came on Pentecost. Some scholars have reasoned that Jesus' birth may have occurred on another Jewish holiday, the Feast of Tabernacles, or *Sukkot,* on the 15th of Tishri (October).

The Feast of Tabernacles or *Sukkot* was the celebration when families would make small huts and camp out in them for seven days. *Sukkot* is one of the three major holidays that were pilgrim festivals, when the Jews traveled to the temple in Jerusalem. The word *Sukkot* means booth or hut. Camping out in these small huts was a reminder of a life in tents during the forty years of Sinai wilderness wandering. Imagine the excitement experienced by each family as they planned to live outside for a week! "…the Lord your God will bless you in all your produce and in all the work of your hands, so that you shall be altogether joyful" (Deut. 16:15).

Although we cannot know for sure, we do know that it would be in keeping with God's way of working to send His Son—the Word made flesh, who made His "dwelling" or "tabernacle" among us (John 1:14)—on the Feast of Tabernacles, when the Jews lived in temporary dwellings and listened to the Word of the Lord being read (Deut. 31:10–13).

For the Jews, *Sukkot* is "the time of our rejoicing." For all of us, our time of rejoicing is the birth of Christ, who brings the joy of salvation to the entire world. My prayer and hope is that when we celebrate Christmas, we do so with excitement and joy and not with dread and disdain for all of the work that we impose upon ourselves.

The Real Christmas Story

When Mary was told by the angel Gabriel that she was going to carry the Son of God, she willingly submitted to God's plan for her, knowing full well that her life would never be the same. She probably would be an outcast for the rest of her life. Her answer was strong and convicting, "Behold, the bondslave of the Lord; be it done to me according to your word" (Luke 1:38).

Mary carried Jesus into the world, raised Him, and saw Him put to death before her. Those of us who love Jesus with all of our hearts, minds, and souls are in many ways called to do the same. *We are all Marys, carrying Jesus in us for the world to see and hear, for their salvation.* That is how we can honor Jesus on His birthday.

As a fresh reminder of why and what we are celebrating, following is the real Christmas story from Luke 2:1–20:

> Now it came about in those days that a decree went out from Caesar Augustus, that a census be taken of all the inhabited earth.
>
> This was the first census taken while Quirinius was governor of Syria.
>
> And all were proceeding to register for the census, everyone to his own city.
>
> And Joseph also went up from Galilee, from the city of Nazareth, to Judea, to the city of David, which is called Bethlehem, because he was of the house and family of David, in order to register, along with Mary, who was engaged to him, and was with child.
>
> And it came about that while they were there, the days were completed for her to give birth.

And she gave birth to her first-born son; and she wrapped Him in cloths, and laid Him in a manger, because there was no room for them in the inn.

And in the same region there were some shepherds staying out in the fields, and keeping watch over their flock by night.

And an angel of the Lord suddenly stood before them, and the glory of the Lord shone around them; and they were terribly frightened.

And the angel said to them, "Do not be afraid; for behold, I bring you good news of a great joy which shall be for all the people; for today in the city of David there has been born for you a Savior, who is Christ the Lord.

"And this will be a sign for you: you will find a baby wrapped in cloths, and lying in a manger."

And suddenly there appeared with the angel a multitude of the heavenly host praising God, and saying,

"Glory to God in the highest, and on earth peace among men with whom He is pleased."

And it came about when the angels had gone away from them into heaven, that the shepherds began saying to one another, "Let us go straight to Bethlehem then, and see this thing that has happened which the Lord has made known to us."

And they came in haste and found their way to Mary and Joseph, and the baby as He lay in the manger.

And when they had seen this, they made known the statement which had been told them about this Child.

And all who heard it wondered at the things which were told them by the shepherds.

But Mary treasured up all these things, pondering them in her heart.

And the shepherds went back, glorifying and praising God for all that they had heard and seen, just as had been told them."

Jesus came to earth to reveal who His Father is and to conquer death. By believing on His name and the work He did on the cross, we can have eternal life with Him. Romans 10:9–10 explains how a person becomes a child of God: "If you confess with your mouth Jesus as Lord, and believe in your heart that God raised Him from the dead, you shall be saved; for with the heart man believes, resulting in righteousness, and with the mouth he confesses, resulting in salvation".

Christmas is celebrating the fact that God came to earth for us! This first time, He came as a baby. When He comes again, He will come as a King to rule forever! Those who do not accept Him as Lord and Savior will not be received by Him. And although His Word says that all may come to Him, many do not.

Here is a poem by an unknown author that shows what can happen to a person who is not ready when Jesus comes back. It will make you realize how important it is to share the good news of Jesus Christ with everyone:

'Twas the Night Before Jesus Came

"'Twas the night before Jesus came and all through the house, not a creature was praying, not one in the house. Their Bibles were lain on the shelf without care in hope that Jesus would not come there.

The children were dressing to crawl into bed, not once ever kneeling or bowing a head. And Mom in her rocker with baby on her lap, was watching the Late Show while I took a nap.

When out of the East there arose such a clatter, I sprang to my feet to see what was the matter. Away to the window I flew like a flash, tore open the shutters and threw up the sash!

When what to my wondering eyes should appear, but angels proclaiming that Jesus was here. With a light like the sun sending forth a bright ray, I knew in a moment this must be THE DAY!

The light of His face made me cover my head. It was Jesus! Returning just like He had said. And though I possessed worldly wisdom and wealth, I cried when I saw Him in spite of myself.

In the Book of Life which He held in His hand, was written the name of every saved man. He spoke not a word as He searched for my name; When He said, "It's not here," my head hung in shame.

The people whose names had been written with love, He gathered to take to His Father above. With those who were ready He rose without a sound, while all the rest were left standing around.

I fell to my knees, but it was too late; I had waited too long and thus sealed my fate. I stood and I cried as they rose out of sight; oh, if only I had been ready tonight!

In the words of this poem the meaning is clear; the coming of Jesus is drawing near. There's only one life and when comes the last call, we'll find that the Bible was true after all!"

Chapter 10

PLAN TIME TO REFLECT AND PREPARE FOR THE NEW YEAR

I REMEMBER ONE time when I was a little girl and my parents were having a New Year's Eve party. I was so excited and begged to stay up until midnight. I wasn't quite sure why that was so exciting, but everyone else was doing it, so I wanted to also. My mother compromised by saying that at midnight, she would wake me up so I could be a part of the celebration.

I went to bed as promised, believing that I would be able to stay awake easily, but the next thing I knew, my mother was gently waking me up. I can remember to this day how tired I was. I couldn't have cared less about saying, "Happy New Year." I just wanted to go back to sleep.

Now that I'm an adult, I believe that welcoming in the New Year is an important ritual. It's important to say "good-bye" to the old and "hello" to the new. It's also important to examine what needs to be changed and what needs to be added to our lives.

It's important to say "good-bye" to the old and "hello" to the new.

Beginnings are exciting to me! A new year is like opening a brand-new journal full of clean, white paper that is ready to be written on. It's like a new school year with new school supplies. Or watching a wedding and seeing the couple taking vows, which will be the beginning of their new life together.

Some people fear a new year. They fear change. They fear the hardship of making changes in their lives, even if the changes will be positive for them. God understands every emotion we have; He created them! And one reason He came to earth was to show us that He loves us and wants to help us along the path every day. He said, "Fear not, for I have redeemed you; I have called you by your name, you are Mine" (Isaiah 43:1). There is great peace when we realize that God the Father is with us every second of every day. When a new year comes around, He wants us to prepare for it with joy.

So, what is the best way to prepare for a new year? Many people, of course, make resolutions. I think they are very important. But I'd like to go a step further. Perhaps we should make resolutions based on what we want in our lives and what has bothered us in our lives. Preparing for a new year requires smart planning and choosing the right goals for this time in our lives.

However, don't feel pressured to *immediately* make changes. Our bodies are physiologically programmed to make goals and start new things in the spring. Perhaps that's why so many people fail to keep their resolutions. Still, around New Year's is a good time to begin the planning and choosing of your goals for the year.

> *Preparing for a new year requires smart planning and choosing the right goals for this time in our lives.*

First, plan some time for yourself, so you can be alone and reflect on the past year. What has *bothered* you the most: your weight, in-laws, finances, children, home changes, etc.? Then, think carefully about what *you want*. Most people really don't know what they want, but when they find out, it totally can change their lives. Do you want to: work, stay home, cook more, clean less, hire someone to help you, start a new hobby, exercise, read more, etc.?

Plan Time to Reflect and Prepare for the New Year

After you write down your real thoughts and truths, meet with your husband so you both can write down your goals for the new year. I know some husbands don't want to write goals with their wives. Don't let that deter you. Go ahead and write yours and your children's down on paper. The success rate of a goal written down is almost ninety-five percent more than those not written down.

I also encourage writing down specific resolutions rather than vague ones. It is easy to write down that you want to lose weight. But it is better to add a specific way you will be able to achieve that goal. For example, add that your plan is to walk every day for thirty minutes. That way, you will set your walking shoes next to your purse to remind you to walk that day. You also might want to keep a pad of paper and pen in your kitchen and in your purse so you can easily record everything you eat in a day. The resolution to lose weight is now matched with specific steps that will be enormously helpful to you in achieving your goals.

Earlier, I mentioned having your children make resolutions for the new year. One year, my youngest daughter said she wanted to dance in the Denver Ballet's *Nutcracker*. She had mentioned it before, but I hadn't taken her seriously. Once she stated it was her goal for that year, I knew I needed to make some phone calls and see when tryouts where. I found out the tryouts were in a few weeks, and much to my surprise, she made it! If she had never expressed a desire to be in the *Nutcracker*, I would not have taken the steps that helped her attain her goal. I also thought her goal was too high. This taught me a lesson that nothing is too hard for the Lord. Psalm 37:5 says, "Commit your way to the Lord; trust also in Him, and He will do it." Where is our faith as we make our New Year's resolutions? Remember, nothing is impossible for the Lord (Luke 1:37).

Many of us sabotage our own goals. Or they seem too hard and we just stop trying. This time, cover your goals with prayer. Ask the Lord what goals you need in your life. He will let you know. Then pray and ask the Holy Spirit to give you the power to make the changes. Remember that God's ultimate goal for each of us is to be conformed into the image of His Son, Jesus Christ. Let your New Year's resolutions lead you in that direction.

Here are some questions that might help you to develop your resolutions:

1. Is what you are doing in your life working?
2. Are the results of what you are doing in different areas healthy?
3. Are you making everyone happy except yourself?
4. Is the cost of what you are doing or having to live with too high?
5. Are you having problems with anger or bitterness?
6. Are you getting enough rest?
7. Are you too stressed?
8. Are you being spiritually fed?

As you write down the answers to these questions, remember to write down the steps you can take that will help you. If you don't know how to solve some of your major problems, find a counselor at your church who may be able to help.

One thing we can do every day that can totally change our lives is to express gratitude. Being grateful and thankful to the Lord and to others takes the emphasis off of ourselves and is certainly a cure for complaining. In fact, the Father wants His children's lives to be characterized by gratefulness. His Word tells us that a thankful attitude should be evident in our worship, giving, relationships, and reactions to the problems we have day to day. In other words, being thankful to the Lord should permeate everything we do (Romans 14:6).

The Lord actually commands us to be grateful: "Rejoice always; pray without ceasing; *in everything give thanks*; for this is God's will for you in Christ Jesus" (1 Thess. 5:16–18, emphasis mine). Some people don't understand why this should be done. They question it because it doesn't make sense to thank God for the death of a loved one or a lost job or opportunity. But He knows how a grateful attitude affects our hearts. When we thank God, it:

Plan Time to Reflect and Prepare for the New Year

- Keeps us aware of His presence in our lives.
- Reminds us of our total need for Him.
- Focuses us on Jesus Christ, which reduces our pride.
- Makes us look for His purposes in our situations.
- Replaces anxiety with peace and joy.
- Takes our eyes off of ourselves and puts them on Him.

This is why one of my favorite holidays is Thanksgiving. It is fully about expressing thanksgiving and appreciation for so many of the intangible things that give our lives meaning and substance. It reminds me of the words to an old hymn: "Count your many blessings, name them one by one." It would be great to do this every day. In fact, talk show hosts and news stories have expounded on the changes that take place in a person's life when he or she is grateful for as little as five things a day. They also say that keeping a "gratitude journal" will change your life.

Deborah Norville wrote a book called *Thank You Power: Making the Science of Gratitude Work for You*. She compiled psychological and behavioral research and true-life stories that back up her theory: thankfulness leads to fulfillment. One study from the University of California found that when people are grateful, they are more optimistic, more apt to help others, more joyful, and genuinely healthier. Other studies have found that they are more resilient, less stressed, and better strategic thinkers. Deborah was surprised to learn that people may recover faster from trauma and they bounce back more quickly from calamity, such as an attack or horrific car crash. They decided to be thankful, for they believe something better will come from it.

I believe that is why Romans 8:28 is a verse most of us love to remember, "And we know that God causes all things to work together for good to those who love God, to those who are called according to His purpose." We might never know why something has happened, and we might hate that something has happened, but when we accept that God is in control, we can praise His name anyway, knowing that something good will come from it.

Having a grateful heart is one of the most important aspects of the Christian life, for it will prepare us to handle difficult situations and is foundational for contentment, hope, and peace in our lives. During one of the lowest points in King David's life he wrote, "It is good to give thanks to the Lord, and to sing praises to Thy name, O Most High; to declare Thy lovingkindness in the morning and Thy faithfulness by night" (Ps. 92:1–2). David looked at life from a different point of view. Instead of being me-focused, he was God-focused.

As you continue to form your resolutions for the new year, remember to write down "to be grateful and thankful every day"—not just for the holiday season but for every day all year long. Be thankful for each breath you take, because you are alive; for each time you clean your house, because you have a house to clean; for each time you change a diaper or make a meal, because you have a child and family; and for sore muscles, because you have a body that can move.

Here are a few other ideas for your resolutions:

1. Choose to be happy. When one person becomes happy, the chances that a friend, sibling, spouse, or next-door neighbor will become happy increase between eight and thirty-four percent, researchers found.[9]
2. Be aware of your own self-talk. If you constantly put yourself down, you will suffer from it. Be positive.
3. Learn something new daily. Never stop reading or learning, for it will open up new horizons in your life that you never thought possible.
4. Plan to do something that makes you happy once a day, even if it is sitting down with a cup of tea and the mail. If it's something you look forward to, your whole day will be better.
5. Get moving. Yes, you hear this all the time, but it works! Take a walk daily, if at all possible; play with the dog; or shoot hoops with your children.

Plan Time to Reflect and Prepare for the New Year

6. Go outside. Being outdoors in direct sunshine for at least thirty minutes a day is a proven mood lifter.
7. Keep up with your personal hygiene. During times of stress, it's easy to forget the daily work of showers, teeth care, etc. But it is so important to keep yourself clean and presentable.
8. Open up your front door—from the outside. It's good to walk into your home as if you are a guest. You will be able to see areas in your home that need attention—cleaning, painting, decorating, etc. Get some paper and a pen and walk throughout the house, listing what needs to be done to get your home organized.
9. Get a pet! Research shows that pets help lower blood pressure and help you live longer. If you are unable to own one, ask your neighbors if you can walk and play with theirs.
10. Schedule a health and dental checkup.
11. Plan good times! Make a list of friends you want to connect with this year. Schedule date nights with your husband. Plan special times with each child separately. Plan a party where everyone brings a dish so you won't be stressed. And plan at least one vacation (they don't have to be expensive, but you do have to have them). Just remember to have fun each day and to enjoy your life!
12. Eat healthy. Yes, I know it's easier said than done. But let's put it on our New Year's resolution list because we are what we eat. I have tried to start listing what I eat each day, and it has helped me stay on course. I love to drink a coke more than anything, but instead of drinking one every day, I try to limit myself to one a week. I also love potato chips and cookies, but again, I don't buy them at the grocery store. I buy fruit that I really like so that I'll eat it. I try to eat a salad every day and to eat smaller portions. I drink skim milk, eat 100-percent whole wheat, and eat as much fresh food as I can. I also stay away from packaged foods.
13. Rest. This is so important! Along with getting enough sleep each night, we have to have rest times during the day. Try to stop and take deep breaths in mid-morning and

mid-afternoon. Take a breath, hold it to the count of six, and then release it slowly to a count of six. Also, sit away from the computer for five to ten minutes and relax. Or take a break with a quick walk outside or a small snack.
14. Stay financially balanced. Don't spend too much, and don't allow yourself or your family to go into debt. If you are in debt now, make a firm resolution to get out of debt this year. You may need to go to a financial counselor to help you with this. God wants to take care of you, and He can if you allow Him.
15. Balance your time and commitments. It's OK to say "no." Write down your priorities at the beginning of the year and your own mission statement. If something doesn't balance with what you have determined is important, then don't do it. Nothing causes stress more than being overcommitted.
16. Let go of the past. We all have something we wish never had happened in our past. But it is over, and we must forget it and move on. As Philippians 3:13–14 says, "forgetting what lies behind and reaching forward to what lies ahead, I press on toward the goal for the prize of the upward call of God in Christ Jesus."
17. Choose to forgive. The end of a year is a wonderful opportunity for you to engage in earnest reflection. Take time to forgive anyone who has wronged you during the year and those you still harbor resentment or bitterness toward. Begin the new year with a refreshed heart. God tells us to forgive, just as He forgives us. He didn't tell us we would *feel* like forgiving, but just to obey Him (Matt. 6:14-15).
18. Plan time with the Lord in prayer and in His Word each day. Apart from the Lord, we can do nothing (John 15:5).

When we celebrate Christmas and other holidays, it is so easy for us to get drawn into everything that the occasion isn't. Now that you have read this book, take time to reflect on what they mean to you, or rather, what you want them to mean to you.

Plan Time to Reflect and Prepare for the New Year

One of my favorite movies of all time is *It's a Wonderful Life* with Jimmy Stewart. His character, George Bailey, never had much material wealth, and he never got to travel the world, which was his heart's desire. Then, when some money was lost on Christmas Eve, he realized that his small business might go bankrupt and he might land in jail. He completely lost hope, wanting to end his life. Though his enemy tried to convince him that he was better off dead than alive, God revealed the truth through a series of events. And, as those of you who know the story will remember, with the help of an angel, George saw that his life had value after all.

It's the last scene of the movie that gets me every time. His brother, who has just arrived, raises a toast to him and says, "To the richest man in town!" No, he didn't have worldly possessions, but he had a family that loved him and friends that would sacrifice for him. Perhaps that's the real spirit of Christmas, celebrating the love God gave to us to share with others.

God bless you, everyone!

References

Quotations in this book come from the following sources:

1. Dr. Mehmet Oz, M.D., "Shortcuts to Less Stress," (*Good Housekeeping* magazine, November 2006), page 34
2. Dr. Aditya Sharma, "Trim the Hustle and Bustle: Relaxing is the Best Gift Parents Can Give," (*Dallas Morning News*, 2010), page 13
3. Dr. Kay Allensworth, "Stress in America Survey," (*Dallas Morning News*, 2010), page 13
4. Same as #3
5. Sharon Glasgow, "A Simple Christmas," (*Proverbs 31* magazine, December 2010), page 2-3
6. Dr. Charles Stanley, "Families in the Bible," (*In Touch* magazine, December 2006)
7. Dr. Gary Small, M.D., "UCLA Center on Aging Report," (*Good Housekeeping* magazine)
8. Brenna Hall, "The History of the Candy Cane," (*Frisco Style* magazine, December 2005) page 25
9. Nicholas Christakis, "Study Says Happiness Makes the Rounds in World," (*Dallas Morning News*, December 2008) page 8

About the Author

LANE JORDAN IS a best-selling Author, National Motivational and Inspirational Speaker, Recording Artist, Bible Teacher, Certified Professional Life Coach, Wife, Mother and Grandmother. She attended Auburn University, where she studied Fashion Merchandising and Marketing. She then transferred to Georgia State University and graduated with a BA degree in Journalism and Broadcasting.

Lane was born and raised in Atlanta, Georgia, in a family of seven children. As a child, she enjoyed gymnastics, cheering, piano, and scouting. Now that she is an adult, along with her love for reading, writing, and singing, Lane enjoys sports, especially tennis, golf, swimming, walking, and hiking.

Lane served as the associate producer for the weekly television program *In Touch* with Dr. Charles Stanley and was also the editor of the First Baptist Church of Atlanta's weekly newsletter, *The Witness*.

Lane began speaking and writing almost twenty years ago while she was living in Littleton, Colorado. She now lives in Frisco, Texas, with her husband, Scott, who partners with her in ministry. Along with Scott, her family consists of daughter Christi and son-in-law Mike and their daughter Sara; Katie; and Grace.

Lane's heart's desire is to do all she can for the Lord and to love, support, motivate, and encourage women in all walks of life. She has written four books, all on the subject of helping women become more organized. She also released a collection of well-known, contemporary gospel songs titled *How Do I Live?* Currently, Lane writes a weekly blog to help inspire and motivate women in all aspects of their lives. You can find this blog at: www.PathwaysToOrganization.com.

If you are interested in having Lane Jordan speak to your church or organization for seminars, workshops, retreats, special events, or media appearances, you may contact her at:

Lane@LaneJordanMinistries.com
or
www.LaneJordanMinistries.com